mV

G

GREECE, GODS, AND ART

ALEXANDER LIBERMAN

GREECE GODS AND ART

INTRODUCTION BY ROBERT GRAVES

TEXTS AND COMMENTARIES ON THE PHOTOGRAPHS BY IRIS C. LOVE

A STUDIO BOOK

THE VIKING PRESS · NEW YORK

ACKNOWLEDGEMENTS

I wish to acknowledge with gratitude the contribution of Iris C. Love to this project. Her archaeological experience was invaluable in the organization and editing of the material. Her faith, enthusiasm, and knowledge made the final result possible.

In addition I wish to thank Bryan Holme, Peter Kemeny, and Nicolas Ducrot of The Viking Press, for their thoroughness, support, and understanding through the difficulties of realizing this project.

My thanks go to Phyllis Starr, Despina Messinesi, Gladys Pohl, Marcel Guillaume, Ernest Brunner, and especially Edmund Winfield, for their valuable assistance in their fields.

Finally, to my wife, Tatiana, a word of affectionate gratitude for her sustaining presence and inspiration.

ALEXANDER LIBERMAN

In the interest of greater readability, it was felt that footnotes or the formal citation of scholars within the text should be avoided. I would like to acknowledge with gratitude my debt to the following scholars, whose invaluable works I have consulted in the preparation of the texts and captions for this book: Bernard Ashmole, Rhys Carpenter, R. M. Cook, William Bell Dinsmoor, James Walter Graham, Evelyn B. Harrison, Karl Lehmann, Naphtali Lewis, Spyridon Marinatos, George E. Mylonas, Humphry G. G. Payne, Gisela M. A. Richter, Homer A. Thompson, Emily Vermeule.

I would also like to thank Kay B. Maunsbach, whose tactful suggestions have improved these writings.

IRIS C. LOVE

CONTENTS

1461647

THASOS

SAMOTHRACE

MOUNT ATHOS

DELPHI

HOSIOS LOUKAS

OROPUS

DAPHNI

ELEUSIS

CORINTH

ATHENS

OLYMPIA

MYCENAE

EPIDAURUS

TIRYNS

SOUNION

BASSAE

SERIPHOS

DELOS

MYKONOS

PAROS

MISTRA

SIPHNOS

PYLOS

THERA

SCALE — MILES
0   10   20   30   40   50

KNOSSOS

CRETE

INTRODUCTION

Most of the ancient Greeks were farmers in the winter months but became sailors in the summer as soon as the Pleiades had risen. They inherited from the highly civilized Cretans, earlier immigrants of North African and Western Semitic stock, a trade Empire extending on both sides of the Mediterranean from Syria to Spain. Their own ancestry was similarly mixed, including neolithic "aborigines," perhaps also from the Middle East, and Indo-European pastoralists from beyond the Caucasus. But whereas the Cretans had been content with the use of small off-shore islands as trade depots, the Greeks formed a habit of founding colonies dependent on mother cities from which excess of population drove them, myrtle branch in hand. These colonists civilized the barbarous hinterland of the shore they had chosen for settlement.

After thirty years in Spain, France, and other parts of the former Greek Empire—especially Majorca, originally colonized by the Rhodians—and occasional stays in Egypt and Palestine, I at last visited Greece proper: recognizing it at once as the true cultural centre of the Mediterranean. The Greeks have always stubbornly remained themselves despite a long humiliating incorporation in the Roman Empire, the suppression by the Byzantine Church of their ancient worship, exploitation by the greedy Venetians, and nearly five hundred years of barbarous Turkish rule. Somehow they kept their ancient language and alphabet, which is more than one can say of any other Mediterranean people—even Israeli Hebrew is a literary revival, not the native tongue of Palestine since Biblical times. Moreover, Greece had taken over the whole Celestial Empire from Babylon and Egypt, renaming its stars: which still continue Greek despite the attempted intrusion of Roman Emperors, Christian saints, and Moslem heroes. The ancient Greek colony of Iope, later Joppa, now Jaffa, a suburb of Tel Aviv, staged the famous myth of Perseus, Andromeda, Cepheus, Cassiopeia, and Draco, whose story spreads over half the night sky. The constellation Hercules similarly recalls not only the Greek colony of Herculaneum on the slopes of Vesuvius, but the two Pillars of Hercules, now renamed Gibraltar and Ceuta. Berenice, whose hair Father Zeus translated to the Heavens, was a Ptolemaic Greek queen of Egypt.

Since Greece is a small country, broken up by deep gulfs, ridged with criss-cross mountains, and surrounded by many scores of islands, its national spirit was never that of a horde, as among Northern forest peoples, or of subjects to a divine tyranny as in Mesopotamia or Egypt, but a family spirit of independent loosely federated city-states, each with its own government, coinage, armed forces, festivals, customs, myths. Frequent quarrels occurred between states, but they were always kept in the family and seldom fought to the death. The four-yearly Olympic Games Festival imposed a truce even in war. This state of things continued until Alexander the Great, King of Macedon, a semibarbarous state in Northern Greece, decided to conquer the Far East, rather than consolidate the Greek colonial Empire, as his father King Philip—a brilliant military tactician—had intended. So he brought the whole of Greece under his autocratic rule and broke the ancient principle of individuality and diversity, in the name of national cohesion.

Each city-state had guarded its myth of origin as a charter of independence, and honoured its founding heroes. These religious myths were yearly represented in dramatic ballets, a long list of which has been preserved by the historian Lucian. And every local custom had its mythological validation: explaining why, for instance, some clans wore only one sandal, why others were forbidden to eat wild asparagus or trained dolphins for children to ride. Religion was everywhere. No contract could be made, no statue carved, no weapon forged, no vase painted and fired, no building raised, without a religious rite. The twelve Olympian Gods and Goddesses who officially ruled Greece under Father Zeus had begun as ancestral deities of an early All-Greek federation centered in the Peloponnesus. Yet Homer, whose works enjoyed a sort of Biblical sanctity throughout the Greek Empire, had made fun of almost all these Gods except two patrons of the Homeric Guild of travelling minstrels: Apollo and Hermes. Few Greeks could therefore take the Olympian cult seriously, even though it regularized public relations between city-states.

In fact, the Greeks had three interlaced religious systems. These were local worship, the official Olympian cult, and the Mystery cults, such as those of Corinth and Samothrace but especially the Eleusinian cult near Athens. Would-be initiates, who had to be free men with no slave blood in their family histories and without any criminal record, were subjected to long careful screening by priests, then after preliminary induction into the Lesser Mysteries they were taken aside, starved, purged, stripped naked, scared, and, finally, it seems with the help of hallucinogens introduced into the sacred bread and drink, were granted glorious visions of Persephone's Paradise. While still highly suggestible, they learned a secret doctrine of personal morality which would guide them safely throughout life and assure them re-entry, at death, into the same paradise.

Homer had never mocked at either Persephone, her mother Demeter, or the God Dionysus, the three Great Gods of the Mysteries. In fact, we may assume him to have been an initiate. More-over the Athenian theatre came under Dionysus's own patronage; all the playwrights, musicians, and actors will also have been initiates, and the tragedies seem to present conflicts between public morals as condoned by the Olympic code, and the secret doctrine taught at the Mysteries.

As Greece grew more commercial, and political power fell into the hands of men either unqualified or unwilling to undergo the ordeals of the Mysteries, religious feeling dulled. By the late fifth century B.C. mercantilism, philosophic theory, and the mechanical sciences had invaded the territory of religion. Buildings became architecturally formalized; statues, no longer archaically carved by craftsmen in a state of divine possession, were turned out in realistic neo-Persian style by matter-of-fact journeymen sculptors; coins became artistically ingenious playthings, not holy objects. Pottery soon also degenerated into trade-ware mass-produced by slave labour for export to barbarians.

A single event marked the final irrevocable decline of ancient Greek tradition. Alexander, after his unpardonably irreligious destruction of Thebes, one of the holiest and most ancient Greek cities, invaded Asia Minor. Having reached Gordium and there been challenged to unpick the complicated Gordian leather knot—a religious task, that should be accomplished only by divine inspiration—he sneeringly cut it through with his sword. Then he marched for India, in an attempt to outdo the God Dionysus, who had got no further than Bactria, and on returning to Persia died as a result of trying to out-drink his divine rival.

Whenever imperial dictatorship, philosophic theory, schools of art, and commercialism usurp the religious sense, as has happened again in modern Europe and America, one must turn for spiritual refreshment to the unspoilt countryside, or to museums. Or to ruins—the hand of time and the invasion of wild nature can lend even an ugly Roman-provincial building a certain beauty. I am glad to have seen a few remains of the true Greece, before the new wave of touristic commercialism does for them what, for instance, the Shakespeare cult has done for the town of Stratford-on-Avon; or the cult of sun-tan has done for fishing villages of the once-Greek Costa Brava in Spain.

ROBERT GRAVES

To Dolly and Nico Goulandris
A.L.

GREECE, GODS, AND ART

The Greek experience, the voyage, the contemplation of Greek art, help us, like a religious retreat, to clarify and re-examine our thoughts about art and life at a time when the standards and tastes of our own civilization are changing drastically. The journey is not so much a return to the past as the reseeing of our time, and ourselves, in a different and richer perspective. The experience of Greece, the mother of our culture, is one we feel we have known before; there is in us a strange sense of recognition, of belonging. To record these unforgettable imprints on my mind is the purpose of this book. Its succession of images attempts to re-create in the spectator's imagination one exploration of man's creativity through the passage of time.

The separate visions of the sea, the land, the architecture, the sculpture—the full range of the Greek experience—ultimately become welded into one unforgettable whole. This book is the record of a personal attempt at visual meditation. It is not an exhaustive study of art and archaeology; only the art related to worship that can actually be seen in Greece is shown. Much is omitted, but I hope to have communicated something beyond documentation—the mood of each site and epoch that unexpectedly overwhelms one in the presence of the past, still real as if alive. I have attempted to stimulate the reader into experiencing his own personal voyage of the imagination. Perhaps through the comparison of some of man's earlier expressions of worship a structure will emerge, and the message hidden behind some of the images we thought we knew too well may be revealed.

Through the centuries religious inspiration has been the core of Greek art. To present this flow of man's offerings, the images in this book have been grouped using many of the gods, and finally God, as chronological and geographical links between the epochs, the sites, and the works of art. Beginning with the earliest worship of the Earth Mother, the book then focuses on Apollo, the god most intimately associated with two of Greece's oldest and most sacred sanctuaries, Delos and Delphi, both of which had originally witnessed the worship of the great Earth Mother. From Apollo's birthplace on Delos and oracular seat at Delphi, we move on to Zeus, father of the gods, and the magnificence of the greatest Panhellenic sanctuary, Olympia; then to Athena and Athens, the leading Greek city. The next chapter is devoted to Dionysus, Poseidon, Asclepius, Amphiarus, followed by a discussion of the Mystery Religions, which partially inspired certain ideas and practices in Christianity, the subject of the final chapter.

The Greek conception of life, through philosophy, literature, architecture, sculpture, and—above all—myth, became the standard of reference for Western civilization. Levi-Strauss has observed that "the study of myth can help us resolve one of the most irritating problems of the human sciences, a problem that philosophy has discussed for centuries but does not seem to have solved—namely, what is the beautiful?" The Greek artist, in choosing man's own image to symbolize his deepest urges, stirred an archetypal dream of man's purity. But through the passage of centuries, this ideal of creative life lost contact with its impetus, the primeval motivation of the Greeks, and became merely academic. The emasculation of noble and pure ideals by lifeless, meaningless reproduction of canons learned by rote set the stage for the cultural revolution called Romanticism that led to the birth of modern art. The escape of Western man from the stranglehold of the established powers that used the Greek tradition to stifle new thought and expression is one of the historic developments in our cultural evolution. But the break was never with the original Greek achievement; the search for the pure creative act, in harmony with nature, still drives us to seek and study the earliest art of Western civilization.

The artistic concept of purity is a major obsession of our time. There is a religious fervour in this striving to raise man out of his earthbound confusion into the realm of the ideal. It is as if in the execution of art that attempts to be pure the artist seeks a self-cleansing activity. Like the ritual of religion, this is a soul-purifying process.

The voyage back, the return to the birthplace of that art is essential to the creation of a receptive state. Without it there may be no real communion with the creations of the past. As Stendhal found, land, climate, race all contribute to our perception of art, just as they influenced artistic creation itself. Nowhere as in Greece today do successive layers of culture reveal themselves with such clarity. For Greece, in its geographical compactness, is a microcosm; it is comparable to a culture isolated in a laboratory for the study of a virus. In Greece, traces of so many civilizations are preserved in expressive fragments, spanning thousands of years, that one can truly observe and compare, and only then begin to identify the periods when man came closest to the divine. For the Greeks, gods were the very personification of natural phenomena; human fears and awe before incomprehensible power were their deepest motivation.

To see the Greek landscape is to realize one of the reasons for the Greek sense of scale. Distances are short, islands small and numerous; Greece is a land of limits. Her monuments present a scale that never overwhelms; we can perceive and feel without being terrorized into admiration. The experience of seeing is profoundly altered by the quality of light. The light of Greece is perhaps the major discovery an artist can make. It has a piercing, cutting quality that seems to encompass in its illumination impossible extremes of strength and tenderness. It acts like a clear fluid in which we can confront the very particles of objects, as if they were suspended in it. It seems to permit no illusion. It is a light ideal for architecture and its most human expression, sculpture. The vestiges of temples and monuments, sometimes reduced to a few re-erected columns or in many cases only the bare trace of a foundation, demand the involvement of the spectator. The broken columns, the cut and broken stone remnants, become the found objects of a searching aesthetic need and are easily transmutable material for an assemblage in the mind. Seeing Greek art in Greece is an experience in abstraction. Time has removed the colours and ornaments from the temples, but what remains has a tremendous, perhaps even stronger, power of evocation. Our modern minds are exposed to the essential link that underlies all great art—man's need to worship, his awe before the unknown.

Distracted by the clutter of life, the accumulation of so much that is unnecessary, we lose contact with essentials. Religion first, then art at its highest, remind man of life's real meaning and of his human condition. Contemporary painting and sculpture, the most advanced forms of abstraction, have an affinity with the archetypal abstraction of the Greeks. Plato's concept of number underlying visual reality prefigures the geometrically impersonal art that stimulates creative minds today. But Plato is experienced abstractly through words, and it seems to me that a misunderstanding arises that can only be settled by a confrontation with the reality of Greece and Greek visual art. There at the site, a particular variation of a smile on a kouros, of the proportion of a column, render the abstract individual and human. Throughout history that trace of individuality within the grand impersonal concept has separated the true artist from the craftsman. Each great creation is a prayer, each prayer has a different intent; and perhaps only the subtlest can render an infinitesimal part of man's aspiration to speak to God—or to the gods.

Today, when we are conditioned to look for originality, striking innovation, the individual sledge-hammer statement that seems unconnected with any other creation, as if born *sui generis,* the Greek lesson of the importance of the small variation, of subtlety and of a continuation of tradition is revealing and meaningful. No art is born in a vacuum. Even the most startlingly individual discoveries of contemporary art are linked to man's artistic and spiritual evolution. Although we may believe that with each epoch man progresses, something in him remains, apparently, unchanged. The past is not that far from us, nor is primitive or archaic art. Because it is remote in time, it is not less good than that of more recent, and supposedly "more civilized," epochs. One of the great revelations of Greece is the grandeur of her early cultures: Cycladic, Minoan, Geometric, Archaic. The art of these periods expresses an obsession with the fetishistic power of the idol, a vitality that overwhelms all superficial detail. Still linked to the impetus of its archaic sources, the serene nobility of Early Classical sculpture is a high moment of Greek art; the sleek finish, the seductive excess of Hellenistic marbles, comes much later.

I do not believe that we are drawn to the abstraction of Cycladic sculpture only because our sensibilities have been conditioned by modern modes of expression. We are caught by the concept of clarity and intent. In the totemic power of Cycladic marbles the message of worship is communicated without distraction, but within the Cycladic system there is the subtle individual mark of each artist. No two idols are alike. These differences are like the differences between human faces, but within a monumental concept, providing a link between the eternal and the human.

The nobility of form that belonged to the earliest Cycladic works has survived to this day in the cubistic sculptural purity of the Cycladic islands' contemporary architecture, and indeed influenced Le Corbusier. Churches, especially, with their all-white splendour, catch the Greek light on their miraculously interrelated spheres, cubes, and free forms. But I believe that Greece and all

Greek art now have a greater meaning for modern man, a meaning greater than at any other time, because modern art has opened our minds and feelings to a range of experience beyond the simply beautiful. The modern artist strives for a meaning beyond the storytelling subject, a meaning that attempts to reach the myths that are immanent in each civilization and human being. For both ancient and modern man, myth is a means of explaining tragedy, of controlling his awe of violence, destruction, and death. In Greece, everything conspires to intensify the response to myths, rendered visible by her artists, suggesting the hidden meanings of art and life.

In the presence of great art one experiences a sense of the precarious equilibrium between repose and stress that the work embodies. This balance on the brink of the void precipitates a state of contemplation in the mind, and leads it into the realm of mystery. Seeing the havoc wrought by nature, and meditating on the surviving beauty, one becomes aware that destruction itself is a necessary force. Daring to destroy is a vital part of creation. The creative process, in one sense, is a series of destructions. Perhaps it is this process, almost a ritualistic exorcism of the fear of death, that reveals to an artist the vision of survival after death, a suggestion of immortality.

To contemplate ruins is to meditate on the transitory; but, unable as we are to see the future, to understand the timeless patterns, we are reassured by these connections with the past. We may not necessarily find in Greece anything greater than what has been produced in our own or any other time, but we can and do find an art that has faced not only the problems of aesthetics but also social, religious, and philosophical questions—questions that man constantly tries to answer in order to justify his existence. This confrontation of the eternal issue of man's place in a hostile world is the noble essence of Greek culture, which raises its art into the realm of the sublime.

The attempt to approach the divine is the highest aspiration of man, his supreme effort. Art is at its greatest, its most sublime, when the artist, by an unexplained leap of subtle inspiration or divination, brings back from the realm of the unknown a tangible trace of what he has seen or experienced. To look without terror or fear at the present and into the future is one of the daring functions of art. The controlled passion, the clarity of concept, the earthy sense of the human, the wit, the avoidance of aesthetic trickery are all manifestations of the Greek artist's fearless expression of his faith in the triumph of man over the tragic in life.

When we return from Greece, still inwardly glowing with the illumination of the light, "the child of the good," we have experienced a revelation. Greek art in its search for clarity within mystery, for order within the chaos of nature, reaffirms the ultimate purpose of all creative expression, the ennobling of man and life. Without the reminder of these strivings, creation loses its purpose and man's life its meaning. Through the ages, whatever the creed, faith and worship expressed through art have sustained man and opened his eyes and his soul to the sublime beatitudes.

For, in Plato's words, "The soul is like the eye: When resting upon that on which truth and being shine, the soul perceives and understands, and is radiant with intelligence."

ALEXANDER LIBERMAN

The Aegean Sea

1

I

THE GREAT EARTH MOTHER

THE CYCLADES, KNOSSOS, MYCENAE, TIRYNS, PYLOS

... Sing of the mother of all gods and men. She is well-pleased with the sound of rattles and of timbrels, with the voice of flutes and the outcry of wolves and bright-eyed lions, with echoing hills and wooden coombes.

—*To the Mother of the Gods* (Homeric Hymn XIV)

Evidence from Anatolia and from mountain caves on Crete attests to the worship of the great Earth Mother in Neolithic times, the later Stone Age. According to mythology, Gaea, goddess of the Earth, was the mother of Rhea, who was also known as Great Mother and Mother of the Gods. Rhea bore to Kronos the six powerful divinities Zeus, Poseidon, Hades, Hera, Demeter, and Hestia. In Asia Minor, Rhea was sometimes worshipped as the Mountain Mother; on Samothrace she was known by the name of Axeiros and worshipped as the Mother of the Rocks; in Phrygia as Cybele; and in Crete as Mistress of the Beasts, often represented on a mountaintop flanked by two lions. In Mycenaean times she was probably invoked by the name of Potnia (Great Lady), or Matera Teija (Mother of the Gods, or Divine Mother).

Since before recorded history, frenzied dances on mountaintops accompanied by the music of flutes, horns, drums, and cymbals formed a part of the ritual devoted to the honour of Rhea-Cybele. By whatever name she was called, she was worshipped as the all-powerful Nature Goddess, symbol of the procreative powers of nature.

The race and language of Neolithic Greece are still unknown. It was an age in which metal was not generally used; implements were mostly made of stone, bone, and ceramic. Architectural remains are sparse and primitive; no great megalithic stone structures remain in Greece, as they do in western Europe. The earliest houses seem to have been simple (round or rectangular) with roofs made of thatch.

The sculptures left to us from the Stone Age (plate 1) are strange, fascinating statuettes—mostly of female figures, usually fat, some amazingly naturalistic in terms of anatomy, and others quite abstract in form. These figurines are found in Europe, Greece, and Anatolia. Sometimes the females are represented crouching or sleeping, and sometimes—as in the figures from Hacilar in Anatolia—during intercourse, affectionately embracing a male consort one-third their size. Perhaps the figurines were magical charms, representations of a fertility goddess or the Earth Mother, on whose generosity and whims the total existence of such an agricultural society was believed to have depended. In Thessaly such statuettes were found in towns rather than tombs, suggesting belief in the monotheistic idea of the great Earth Mother on which all European cultures around the Mediterranean focused.

Chronologically Greece's Bronze Age, which followed the Neolithic period, is divided into three major epochs: Early, Middle, and Late. These broad eras are subdivided into three periods and according to locations. The Helladic pertains to the mainland of Greece (and Late Helladic is also known as the period of the Mycenaean Age), Minoan pertains to Crete, and Cycladic pertains to the central Aegean islands.

Much archaeological work remains to be done in the Cyclades, for many questions remain unanswered. We do not know how early these islands were settled. Seemingly they were inhabited late in the Neolithic period and do not appear to have developed a culture until Early Helladic II, *c.* 2500–2200 B.C. The Cycladic civilization persisted untroubled by any serious disasters until the end of the Bronze Age. The Cycladic peoples had three main occupations: maritime trade, farming, and mining.

Scholars have demonstrated that the Cycladic peoples engaged in commerce with people on the mainland, at times even living and intermingling with them. Cycladic exports are found in many areas of the Mediterranean world—from Anatolia to Sicily, and from Bulgaria to Crete—impressive evidence of an intrepid, enterprising people.

Remnants of Cycladic architecture, though known, are sparse. Only three village sites have been excavated: Phylakopi on the island of Melos; Santorini (ancient Thera); and Chalandriani on Syros, where ruins of a developed fort were found. However, the typical Cycladic two-room houses, constructed of rock and slate without brick or plaster, no longer exist.

Over two thousand Cycladic graves have been noted. In these graves—among tweezers, "sauce-boats," enigmatic "frying pans," pins, needles, and cockleshells—were found the idols of these people. Similar statuettes have also been found in many areas of the Mediterranean, where they were locally imitated.

The religious significance of these statuettes is uncertain. There are three main types: the typical idol, usually a female with arms folded under her breasts; the flatter "violin-shaped" idols; and groups, either one figure supporting another on its head, or musicians such as are shown in plates 3 and 4. They vary in size from eight inches to five feet. Not every tomb excavated has produced one, but sometimes several idols are found in one grave with only one skeleton.

They are quite different in conception and variations from the ubiquitous fertility goddess of the Neolithic Age. Presumably the larger of the Cycladic idols had had a function before being placed in the graves, since some of the statues were deliberately broken in order to fit them into the tomb. Surely the smaller figurines were more than decorative ornaments—but exactly what they were meant to represent remains unknown. The religious practices of the Cycladic islanders are also a mystery. The omnipotent, all-pervading Earth Mother of the Neolithic period seems to have been temporarily eclipsed, but by whom and for what is still unclear.

About as little is known about the Minoan religion. No monumental images or temples of this cult remain, as they do from the Classical period in Greece; all that can be traced are small sanctuaries or special cult rooms in the palaces reserved for religious practices. The Earth Mother was mainly a nature deity, worshipped outdoors in grottoes, groves, and caves, and on mountaintops. Judging from the snake tubes, stepped altars, tables for liquid offerings, votive double axes, horns of consecration, shrine models, and the dove-goddess and snake-goddess images, religious practices must have been fairly complex. The bull and the symbol of the chthonic powers, the snake, were apparently highly revered.

Still less is known about the religion of the Mycenaeans, although it has generally been considered that they adopted Minoan practices. No definite proof of this exists, and in any case it is unlikely that Minoan religious beliefs would have influenced the Mycenaeans until the latter became the rulers of Knossos around 1400 B.C. Next to nothing of the public religious buildings of the Mycenaean period is preserved, and it may be that ritual practice did not require separate shrines; indeed, the palaces had portable as well as fixed altars. Scant remains of what may have been sacred buildings or altars are known from Keos, Delos, Delphi, Pylos, Mycenae, Epidaurus, and Eleusis.

The famous Linear B tablets excavated at Knossos, Mycenae, and especially at Pylos would seem to document such Mycenaean deities as Potnia Atana (Lady Athena), Hera, Zeus, Enyalios (the Battle God, Ares), Artemis, Poseidon the Earthshaker, Hermes, and Dionysus. In some instances the tablets mention the offerings that were made to the gods: Poseidon, for example, as apparently the patron deity of Pylos, received oil, boars, sows, bulls, sheep, rams' fleece, grain, wine, cheese, and honey.

The earliest representations of deities on the mainland exist on engraved gold rings and gems dating back to the shaft graves of the *Tholos* period. In iconography and style these are Minoan and therefore do not contribute much to the knowledge of Mycenaean religion per se. The majority of images preserved are female, executed in terra cotta, of the so-called *phi* or *psi* type (corresponding to the shape of those Greek letters), and they may well represent various Potnias.

The primary form of Mycenaean ritual seems to have been the sacrifice and burning of animals, as described by Homer. Since Homer lived some four hundred years after the great Mycenaean palaces had fallen, we do not know whether he was writing about Mycenaean traditions or whether he was influenced by the current practice of his day. Essentially, however, these animal sacrifices seem to differ from Minoan ritual, for there is little evidence that the nature-adoring Cretans actually made burnt and blood offerings to their gods (although it has been suggested that after the bull-vaulting games the bull may have been sacrificed as part of their religious ritual).

The history of the Palace of Minos at Knossos begins in the Neolithic period. The area where the palace later stood was the site of one of the largest Neolithic settlements in the eastern Mediterranean world. These first settlers, like the later Minoans, are believed to have come from Anatolia and, ultimately, Asia.

Towards the end of the Middle Minoan period (c. 1700–1600 B.C.), sumptuous palaces and mansions such as Phaistos, Mallia, Kato Zakro, and Knossos were constructed on Crete. The first palace at Knossos, dating from the Middle Minoan period, was destroyed early in the seventeenth century B.C. (whether by the Mycenaeans or by an earthquake is not certain), but it was rebuilt later in an even more grandiose manner. The most brilliant artistic period was the Late Minoan I Age (1600–1500 B.C.), and except for Knossos it was the last in which the building of great palaces can be traced. Various theories regarding the end of this fabulous era have been proffered by archaeologists, and perhaps the most plausible one is that in about 1500 B.C., the island of Thera (modern Santorini) was subjected to a violent volcanic eruption. The shocks created tidal waves that engulfed the coast of Crete, only thirty miles away, destroyed entire towns as well as the palaces, and may have been the origin of the legend of the lost continent of Atlantis.

That there was such an eruption on Thera has been substantiated by recent geological and archaeological evidence—lately incremented by new excavations on a Minoan site on Thera, Akrotiri, apparently a flourishing city of some thirty thousand inhabitants that was suddenly overwhelmed by a volcanic eruption around 1500 B.C., and also by evidence from the Minoan palace of Kato Zakro on Crete, also destroyed at that time, where pots have been excavated containing volcanic ash and pumice. Knossos, located three miles from the sea and shielded by hills, was not destroyed, but it was damaged, and repairs were made to it around 1400 B.C.

An archaeological feud still rages as to whether Knossos was finally destroyed in 1400 B.C. or in 1200 B.C. According to myth, Theseus, a young Mycenaean prince, overthrew King Minos and destroyed his palace at Knossos, taking with him the princess Ariadne. Whether by force or dynastic marriage, both of which are reflected in the Theseus legend, a definite change in artistic spirit certainly took place at Knossos around 1400 B.C. The frescoes decorating the Throne Room of the Palace (see plate 11) contain griffons—foreign to Minoan culture but common in Mycenaean art—in stiff and stylized renditions that can be compared favourably to those in the frescoes at the Mycenaean Palace of Nestor at Pylos, dating some hundred and fifty years later. Further, the gay garden and maritime scenes so characteristic of Minoan art now gave way to stylized heraldic scenes, sometimes with military overtones. Horses and chariots, military equipment of mainland types, appear in certain graves that have been unearthed. In architecture, *tholos* tombs (underground beehive tombs) made their appearance, and in ceramics "Palace style" vases and Mycenaean ceramic imports have been found that link Knossos with the Mycenaean mainland. Perhaps the most important, and certainly the most fascinating, evidence is provided by the Linear B tablets that Michael Ventris brilliantly proved to be written in an archaic form of Greek. These tablets support the theory that the Mycenaean Greeks were in control of Knossos before the palace was totally destroyed, but they do not indicate at what time or by whom. The ruin of the Minoan palaces (with the exception of Knossos) around 1500 was followed immediately by the rise of several Mycenaean centers on the mainland under the suzerainty of Mycenae.

Since it was first erected around 1250 B.C., the famous Lion Gate has remained in full view of those who lived at Mycenae, and today the lions still stand as symbolic guardians of the city. Mycenae had been inhabited since the Early Bronze Age (Early Helladic period 2500–1900 B.C.), and the dramatic growth of its prosperity between 1580–1500 B.C. is suggested by the incredible wealth of gold and precious objects that have been found in its shaft graves. In government and culture, Mycenae became the centre of the Mycenaean world after about 1400 B.C., and its traders and colonists expanded in all directions—towards Anatolia, Syria, Egypt, Sicily, and Italy. It remained a great power for some two hundred years, at which time its cities were destroyed, either by internal conflicts or by the Dorian invasions that began about 1200 B.C. and continued into the following century.

The Dorians, who were of Indo-European Greek stock with a comparatively undeveloped culture, entered Hellas via the Balkan peninsula. They may or may not have been directly responsible for the destruction of all the Mycenaean palaces and towns. In any event, only Athens appears to have totally escaped their colonization or destruction.

It remains something of a mystery how and why all the Mycenaean palaces, most of which were protected by impregnable walls and elaborate fortification systems, fell one after another in such quick succession. It has been suggested that severe droughts may have driven the starving populace to storm the palace where the granaries and remaining food stores were kept. It has also been suggested that the Dorian armies may have been aided by the ubiquitous "sea peoples" who had managed to create such havoc along the Anatolian, Syrian, and Egyptian coasts. The "sea peoples" are mentioned in the fourteenth century B.C. Amarna letters of the Egyptians, and their numbers grow after 1300 B.C., the zenith of the Mycenaean Empire. At the battle of Kadesh, won by the Egyptian Pharoah Rameses II in 1286 B.C., the "sea peoples" are known to have fought on both sides, and it seems obvious that these bands of people, originating in different ethnic groups, not only were knowledgeable in seacraft but enjoyed no unifying loyalty and had strong mercenary and piratical tendencies.

After the devastation of their towns and palaces, the Mycenaeans were pushed back to the sea perhaps by the Dorians and, after taking to boats, escaped to the islands and to the coast of Asia Minor. A few remained behind, and others were to return to their lands later and mingle and intermarry with the Dorians. Whatever the reason, whether it was the Dorian invasions, internal political intrigues, or severe droughts that put an end to the brilliant Mycenaean era, civilization was soon to re-emerge, in the so-called Geometric period—the era of Homer.

NOTES ON THE ILLUSTRATIONS

1 A violin-shaped neolithic terra-cotta figurine, probably representing the goddess of fertility, found at Knossos. Originally, the zigzag design incised across her breast and stomach was undoubtedly filled with pigment. Similar violin-shaped figurines are found throughout Anatolia. (4000–3000 B.C. Heraklion Museum, Crete.)

2 A promontory of the Cycladic island Siphnos, seen from Kastro.

3 "The Flute Player." This masterpiece of Cycladic art (and "The Harp Player," plate 4) was found in a tomb on the island of Keros. The figure exemplifies the abstraction of form that has attracted contemporary interest to Cycladic art. (2400–2200 B.C. Parian marble. National Museum, Athens.)

4 "The Harp Player," of equal quality. The bard, his head thrown back in the ecstasy of the song, is seated on a chair whose intricate form echoes the shape of his harp. (2400–2200 B.C. Parian marble. National Museum, Athens.)

5 Octopus amphora. Cretan artists never decorated their vases with human figures or specific scenes. Fauna and flora were their main inspiration. Most cherished of all the marine animals were the nautilus, the squid, and the octopus. Here the octopus has been somewhat stylized, its tentacles forming a symmetrical composition. Earlier renditions of the subject were freer and more natural. This particular amphora may have been imported from the mainland. (c. 1450–1400 B.C. Heraklion Museum, Crete.)

6 "The Snake Goddess," brandishing a snake in each hand, perhaps symbolized domination over nature and the afterlife. In antiquity the snake represented the renewal of life, because its home was in the earth and annually it shed its skin. Perched on her head is a seated leopard, symbolizing her command of the wild forces of nature. Whether this idol actually represents the Earth Mother or one of her priestesses is a matter of debate. She and other votive offerings were found among two repositories in the main sanctuary of the Palace of Minos at Knossos. Made of faïence (enamelled terra cotta), she is dressed in the manner of a fashionable lady of the Minoan Court. (c. 1500 B.C. Heraklion Museum, Crete.)

7 Ancient Thera, now the island of Santorini (named after St. Eirene). The extraordinary formation that rises out of the sea formed part of the volcanic crater that is now the bay of Thera (see also plate 119). This still-active volcano, one of the legendary forges of the god Hephaestus, almost destroyed the island in an eruption of around 1500 B.C. that ruined the Minoan palaces on Crete by creating a tidal wave, shock waves, and rains of ash and pumice.

8 The Palace of King Minos at Knossos, looking out from the veranda of the Queen's Hall. The floor of the room was white gypsum, and the stuccoed walls were painted with scenes of marine life and dancing figures. In the small bathroom opening immediately off the Queen's Hall, fragments of a clay bathtub were found. The Minoan column, unlike the Classical Greek, tapered downward. The wooden shafts and capitals were usually painted in alternating colors as in these examples restored by Sir Arthur Evans, showing black shafts and red capitals. The shafts were usually smooth, although there is some evidence of fluting and spiralling, and sometimes they were oval instead of round. (c. 1500 B.C.)

9 Looking across the large pillared hall towards the northern entrance (or *propylon*) of the Palace of Minos at Knossos. Some of the original square pillars are visible in the foreground. It has been suggested that the hall served as a market area (*agora*), a customs house, a banquet room, or possibly even a waiting room. Since the great deposit of Linear B tablets was found here, perhaps it served as an archive. The semi-restored colonnade of the propylon shields the stuccoed relief of a charging bull. The palace, with its unbelievably complicated plan, numerous corridors, staircases, and stairwells, is like the labyrinth of the Theseus legend itself. The name "labyrinth" derives from the place of the sacred double-axe, the labrys. The myth of the monster, the Minotaur, half-man, half-bull, could have originated from the priest-kings (Minos) who at times may have donned a ritual bull's mask while officiating at religious and state services, and from the dangerous ritual sport of bull vaulting that the Minoans indulged in and represented so often in their art. (c. 1500 B.C.)

10 Examples of Linear B tablets, deciphered by Michael Ventris in 1953. The tablets deal with palace and land administration, palace and tomb inventories, land allotment, religion, and military and naval strategic plans. They were originally made of unbaked clay; ironically, the fires that destroyed the palaces of Knossos and Pylos baked them, thereby preserving them for posterity. (1230–1200 B.C. National Museum, Athens.)

11 Throne Room, the Palace of Minos at Knossos.

The gypsum throne found *in situ* by Sir Arthur Evans is the oldest in Europe. Its arc forms are similar in spirit to those of the Cycladic "Harp Player" 's chair (plate 4). The heraldic griffons which guard the throne were of Near Eastern origin; although alien to the Minoan repertory, they were at home in Mycenaean works. A fresco similar in subject matter as well as style was found in Nestor's Palace at Pylos. (*c.* 1400 B.C.)

12 The Sarcophagus from Hagia Triada. This scene is taken from one of the sides of the famous sarcophagus found in a tomb at the Minoan Royal Villa. It is made of limestone and was decorated with religious frescoes, perhaps pertaining to the cult of the dead.

A priestess pours a libation into a crater placed between two sacred double-axes, labrys (each surmounted by a bird), possibly a symbolic image of the great Earth Mother. The second figure probably represents the wife of the deceased, and is followed by a lyre player and an acolyte carrying the sacrifice. (*c.* 1400 B.C. Heraklion Museum, Crete.)

13 The Sarcophagus from Hagia Triada. Since it is not certain whether the Minoans made blood sacrifices, the scene from the opposite side shown here—a priestess preparing to sacrifice an ox to the accompaniment of a flute player—may suggest the influence of Mycenaean funeral rituals. Did the sarcophagus contain the body of a Mycenaean prince?

14 A bronze statuette of a young shepherd carrying a sheep for sacrifice. Although the work dates from the early sixth century B.C., the shepherd's costume is strikingly similar to Minoan loincloths. This kind of image, persisting into the Christian Era, eventually became that of the Good Shepherd. (Heraklion Museum, Crete.)

15 The Mycenaean "Triad of Divinities," which may represent two divine nurses rearing a child god, perhaps Zeus. This masterpiece of ivory carving was found in the palace at Mycenae. Nearly all Mycenaean ivories are relief plaques and rare, indeed, is the discovery of a statue in the round. Raw ivory was imported from Syria and eastern ports, and with it came Oriental influences. (*c.* 1350 B.C. National Museum, Athens.)

16 The first view the visitor has of the citadel of Mycenae. Mycenae was founded, according to Pausanias, "because in that site the cap [*myces*] of his [Perseus's] scabbard had fallen off, and he regarded this as a sign to found a city." Pausanias also wrote that Perseus, being thirsty, "chanced to take up a mushroom [*myces*] and that water flowing from it he drank and being pleased gave the place the name

of Mycenae." But King Perseus's dates are placed between 1350 and 1330 B.C., and modern excavation indicates that Mycenae has been inhabited since approximately 2500 B.C.

17 A gold drinking cup (*rhyton*) in the form of a lion's head, found in Royal Shaft Grave No. 4 at Mycenae together with two other rhyta: a silver bull's head (with a golden rosette on its forehead) and a silver stag. The style of this cup reappears later in Scythian art. Drinking vessels in the shape of lions' and bulls' heads are also found in Egyptian tomb paintings (also see plate 23). (1580–1500 B.C. National Museum, Athens.)

18 The Lion Gate and rampart walls of Mycenae. The wall above the lintel of the gate was constructed to form an open triangle, characteristic of Mycenaean architecture and known as the "relieving triangle," so called because the empty space created by the false arch relieved the lintel from bearing the enormous weight of the gigantic stones. This area was blocked by the well-known limestone relief representing two heraldic lions. Their heads were executed in another material, perhaps bronze or steatite. At this gate, Queen Clytemnestra may have greeted the victorious Agamemnon, and through it passed Orestes to avenge the murder of his father. The enormous wall blocks so amazed the Greeks of the Classical period that they attributed their construction to the Cyclops. (1300–1250 B.C.)

19 Dagger from Mycenae. Inlaid with gold, silver, electrum, and niello, this dagger is one of the most famous examples of metalwork found in the shaft graves. The metalwork technique originated in the Near East but continued in Greece. The hunting scene was a favourite theme in Mycenaean art, and this example is the most complex in design of all the sword blades that have been found. (*c.* 1600–1550 B.C. National Museum, Athens.)

20 Mycenae. The lion relief is visible in the foreground, and behind it lies the famous Grave Circle A, discovered by Heinrich Schliemann. The grave circle contains six shafts in which were buried nineteen people and a group of Middle Helladic inhumations. Before the rampart circuit walls and Lion Gate were built (these were two hundred to two hundred fifty years later), the grave circle formed the centre of a large, prehistoric cemetery. The wealth of gold and precious objects excavated here gave a new and real meaning to the Homeric epithet "Mycenae Rich in Gold" (Polychrysos). Beyond the circle and the walls of Mycenae stretches the Argive plain, gateway to the Peloponnesus.

21 A Mycenaean *phi*-type figurine. Such terra-cotta

statuettes of women are found all over the mainland and are generally distinguished as *psi* or *phi* type. Sometimes these figurines hold a child; sometimes they ride in chariots or on donkeys; sometimes they sit on thrones. Do they represent the great goddess, the Lady Potnia or Matera Teija, the mother of the gods? Are they, when they hold children, divine nurses such as the god Zeus was brought up by, or are they ex-votos representing the worshippers themselves? (1350–1200 B.C. Nauplia Museum.)

22 Funeral mask from a shaft grave in Mycenae containing three men and two women. According to Professor Emily Vermeule, the shaft graves represent a departure from previous burial customs in the following respects: "multiple gifts and bodies, carved stelai, the passion for being buried under a heap of gold armour or masks—a child might be dressed completely in gold...." The practice of using funeral masks existed at various periods in Anatolia, Egypt, Bulgaria, and Etruria. (1580–1550 B.C. National Museum, Athens.)

23 One of the two gold *repoussé* Vapheio cups. The cups found at Vapheio, near Sparta, are the only representations of their type that have been preserved. Similar cups appear in Egyptian wall paintings and were inventoried on Linear B tablets. The subject of the two cups, the hunting, trapping, and mating of bulls (here the bull is caught in a net), was clearly of interest to Minoans, but is not found elsewhere in their art; the usual Minoan subject involving men and bulls was bull vaulting, which seems to have had a ritual and sacred meaning. Hunting scenes were more appealing to Mycenaean tastes, yet the splendid modelling and the softness and fluidity of style speak for a Minoan origin. Perhaps, therefore, the cups were made by Minoans to suit Mycenaean tastes. The cups were found in a tholos tomb belonging to a Mycenaean prince who was, according to Tsountas, of effete taste, inasmuch as his body was found surrounded by rings. Gems were found at either of his wrists, eighty amethyst beads on his breast. A mirror, an ear pick, and perfume vases were also part of the tomb furnishings. The cups were placed near his hands. (c. 1500 B.C. National Museum, Athens.)

24 Corbelled Gallery at Tiryns, the "City of Towers," near Mycenae. The gallery is thirty-three yards long, two yards wide, and four and one-third yards high. In time of war it served as a shelter for the townspeople, and in time of peace it was used as a storage area. (c. 1350–1250 B.C. National Museum, Athens.)

25 Heads from a Mycenaean bowl. These heads made as appliqué decorations for a bowl were found at "sandy" Pylos, the site of the Palace of King Nestor. They are made of niello, electrum, gold, and silver. (1250–1200 B.C.)

Goblet, known as "Nestor's Cup." "An exceedingly beautiful cup . . . studded with golden rivets. There were four handles on it, and around each two doves were represented as if feeding, while below there were two supports . . ." (*Iliad*, Book 11, lines 632–37). Thus does Homer describe a cup belonging to King Nestor, the son of Neleus, King of Pylos; while excavating the graves at Mycenae, Schliemann thought he had found this very cup. (1650–1550 B.C. National Museum, Athens.)

26 A section of the round hearth from the Megaron at the Palace of Nestor at Pylos. The Megaron, with its large, round, thick hearth, was the spiritual center of the Mycenaean palace. At Pylos there was a portable altar which stood by the hearth, where the priest or king or priest-king presided over sacrificial rituals. Here the hearth was decorated with a pattern of flames and spirals. It was apparently kept in good repair, for there is evidence of several replasterings and repaintings. The Megaron as an architectural form may be the remote ancestor of the later Greek temple. (1250–1200 B.C.)

27 Tholos tomb at Pylos. Tombs such as this, shaped like a beehive, represent an architectural tradition dating back to the seventeenth century B.C. Tholoi tombs were usually family vaults, and they often had shaft graves or chamber tombs sunk within them. They were constructed so that they could easily be reopened. The Mycenaeans apparently repeatedly opened their tombs and often unceremoniously swept deceased relatives against rear or side walls to make space for a new occupant. The door would be closed again and a farewell toast drunk, after which the cup would be smashed against the door or dropped in the passageway. (c. 1250–1200 B.C.)

28 Bronze votive figures from Crete. A warrior is shown with drawn bow and arrow in a fully manned ship. These charming offerings are not unlike the votive gifts that are still dedicated in Greek churches and Christian sanctuaries throughout the world. (Eighth century B.C. Heraklion Museum, Crete.)

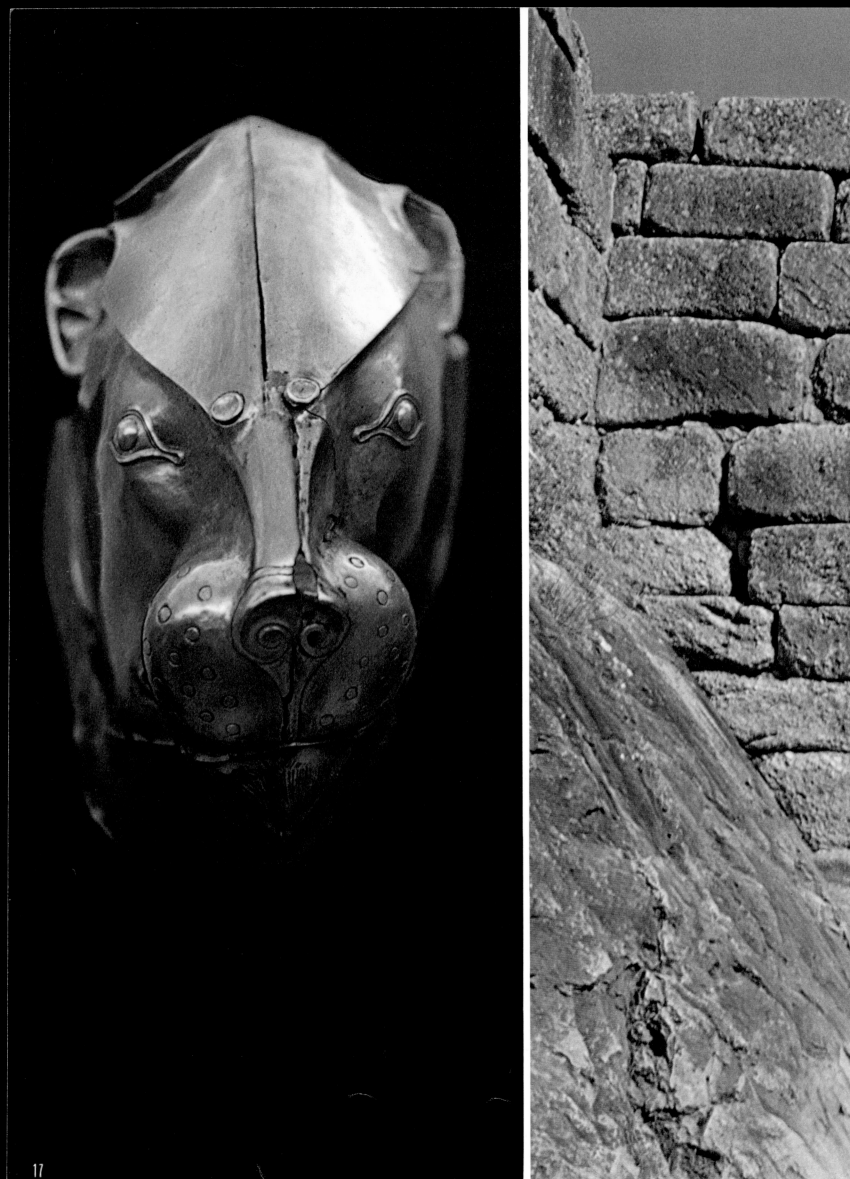

17

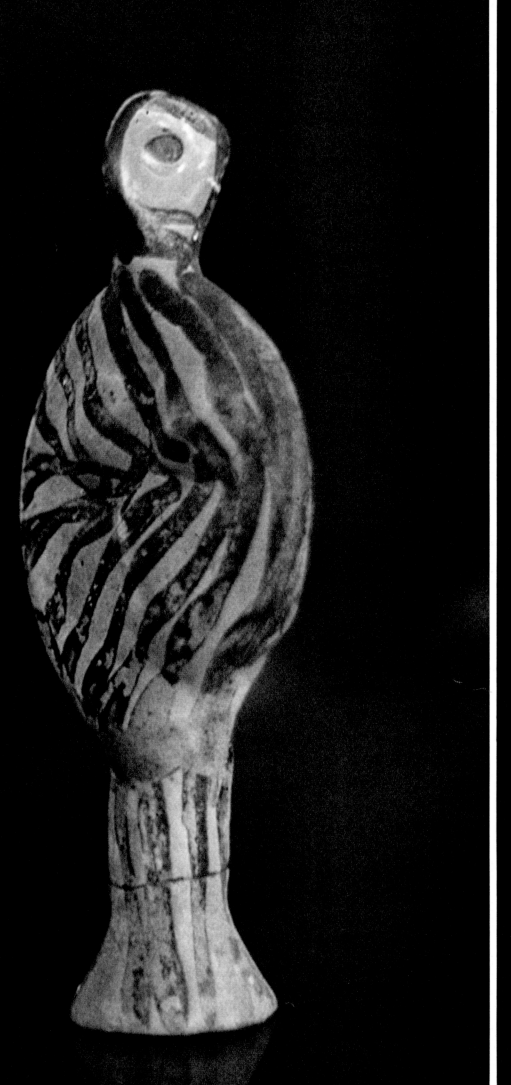
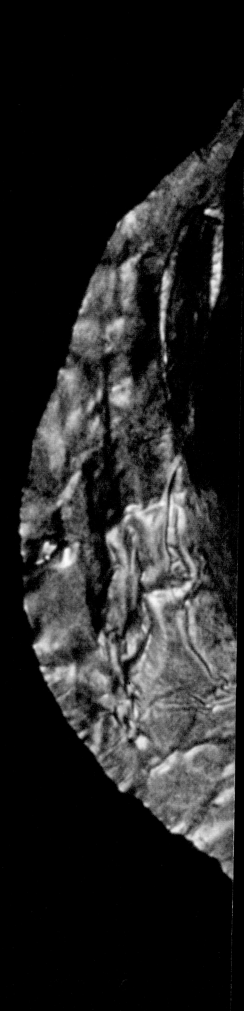

24

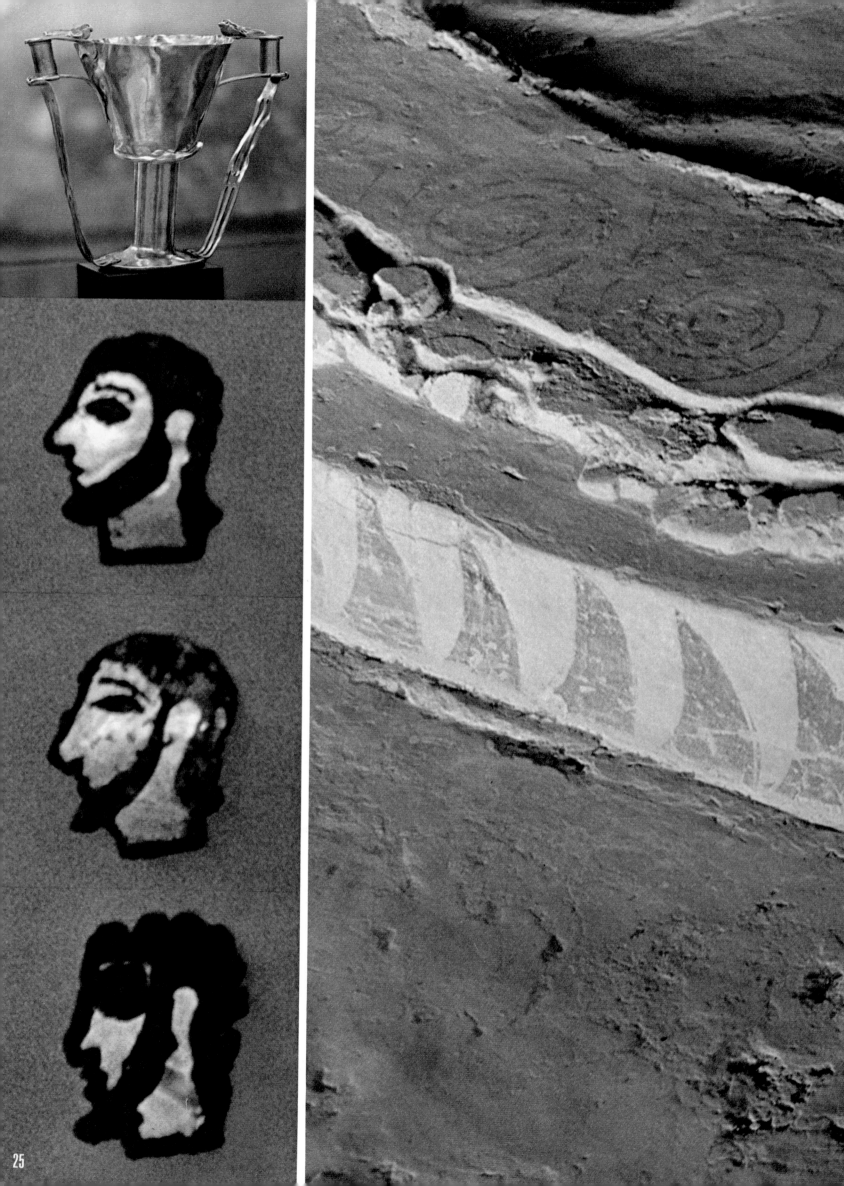

II

APOLLO
DELOS, DELPHI, CORINTH, BASSAE

. . . On Delos, the pains of birth seized Leto, and she longed to bring forth; so she cast her arms about a palm tree and kneeled on the soft meadow while the earth laughed for joy beneath. Then the child leaped forth to the light, and all the goddesses raised a cry. . . .
—*To Delian Apollo* (Homeric Hymn III)

The origin and functions of Apollo are multiple and complex. Originally he may have been an Asiatic, Hittite, or Nordic deity. In Greece he became primarily a solar god (without being the sun itself, Helios), and was credited with the power of making the fruits of the earth grow. He was a god of medicine, but his arrows could also destroy. He was worshipped as the god of youth (young men cut off and dedicated their forelocks to him when coming to manhood); he was the god of music and song, the god of constructions and colonization. Most important, he was the god of divination and prophecy through whom Zeus made his will known. He was honoured by temples and sanctuaries throughout Greece and Asia Minor.

It is interesting that the island of Delos should have been selected by the Greeks as the birthplace of Apollo and his twin sister Artemis, virgin goddess of the hunt, of wildlife, and of childbirth. Delos, Keos, and the sanctuary of Eleusis alone can lay claim to being cult centers that reach back in unbroken sequence at least into the Mycenaean period. A very ancient building, possibly of sacral character, has been found under the archaic sanctuary dedicated to Artemis on Delos. The site may have been relaid when the archaic building was constructed. Gold, ivory, bronzes, seals, and potsherds were found dating from the Mycenaean, Geometric, and Orientalizing periods.

Although Delphi cannot yet claim the honour that Delos does of being one of the three religious centres which date from the Mycenaean through the Classical periods in unbroken sequence, one must remember that Delphi is just as venerable, if not more so. Delphi possesses a Minoan ritual rhyton in the shape of a lioness's head similar to the one found at the Palace of Minos at Knossos. Furthermore, Mycenaean sherds and statuettes, perhaps representing the great Earth Mother, were excavated from under the east flank of the temple of Apollo. It is tempting, too, to give credence to the mention in the Pythian Hymn to Apollo that this god selected, or rather kidnapped, Cretan mariners to become the priests and ministers of his temple at Delphi. Legend has it that, four days after his birth on Delos, Apollo came to Delphi. After shooting the guardian dragon, Python, he took possession of the oracular seat for himself. Through his priestess, the Pythia, Apollo uttered prophecies received from his father, revealing Zeus's will to mankind.

The area of Delphi, perhaps owing to its seismic activity as well as to its great beauty, has always retained an aura of sanctity. Apollo was not the first god to possess the sanctuary. Originally it belonged to the great Earth Goddess, Gaea, and then to her daughter, Themis, goddess of justice. The connection with the Earth Mother is understandable, since there was volcanic activity here and the vapours could be construed as emanating from her "body." It was over a crevice that supposedly penetrated the very depths of Gaea's bosom that Apollo's temples were ultimately constructed. The vapours, the breath of the Earth Goddess, were inhaled by Apollo's priestess, the Pythian oracle, and these inhalations, coupled with the narcotic action of the bay or laurel leaves which she chewed, contrived to put her into a state of ecstasy. Her frenzied words were interpreted by the priests of Apollo, who rephrased the prophecies and gave ambiguous answers to waiting pilgrims.

Mount Parnassus, rising behind Apollo's sanctuary, was first dedicated to his younger brother, Dionysus, and his followers, the Thyiades (Maenads) who ranged the countryside. Later, every five years, clothed in animal skins and armed with their *thyrsoi* (staves topped by pine cones) and torches, they celebrated the mysterious rites of Dionysus (see Chapter V).

NOTES ON THE ILLUSTRATIONS

29 "Apollo." From the east frieze of the Treasury dedicated by the islanders of Siphnos to Apollo in his sanctuary at Delphi. He is seen turning round to listen to his mother, Leto; Artemis's hand is in the background. Apollo's sister and mother are gesticulating, evidently engaged in an animated discussion, probably about the Trojan War. (530–525 B.C. Parian marble. Delphi Museum.)

30 Lion (detail), from the processional avenue of Delos. The muzzle and body of the animal have been smoothed by centuries of weathering. (Seventh century B.C. Naxian marble.)

31 Delos. A view towards the sacred port from the ruins of the residential section near Mount Cynthus.

32 Lions at Delos. Originally, lions faced each other from either side of the avenue. Such a sacred road, lined with statues of seated priests and crouching lions, also leads from Miletus to the temple of Apollo at Didyma. Similar processional avenues (with lions, rams, and sphinxes) existed in Egypt. These lions are among the earliest remaining examples of Greek rounded monumental sculpture. (Seventh century B.C. Naxian marble.)

33 View towards Mount Cynthus, Delos. The reconstructed Doric temple was built by the Athenians and dedicated to the Egyptian goddess, Isis, around 150 B.C. After Alexander's conquest of the Middle East, many foreign deities were introduced into the Greek pantheon.

34 Delphi. The road from Arachova, that follows the ancient sacred way to Delphi; in the foreground is the *Marmaria* (the Marbles; see caption 38). This renowned spot has been inhabited and held sacred since the beginning of the second millennium B.C.

35 Pediment (detail) from the Siphnian Treasury, Delphi, depicting the myth of Heracles, who attempted to steal from Apollo the sacred tripod upon which the Pythia sat while uttering the oracular statements. The scene shows Athena (or Zeus) attempting to act as mediator. The myth may reflect an attempt by the invading Dorians to supplant the worship of Apollo with their own god, Heracles. (530–525 B.C. Limestone. Delphi Museum.)

36 Delphi. The sacred olive trees are like a green sea flowing towards the bay of Itea. The modern town of Itea was built on the site of ancient Krissa, where pilgrims arrived from all over the ancient world.

37 "Cleobis and Biton" by Polymedes. Herodotus wrote, "The Argives made statues of them in Delphi because they were among the most virtuous of men." These youths (*kouroi*) are among the first Greek monumental stone sculptures of human figures executed in the round. (600–590 B.C. Delphi Museum.)

38 The Marmaria, Delphi, the Sanctuary of Athena Pronaea (which may be interpreted Athena, Guardian of the Temple, or Athena, Goddess of Forethought). There was a succession of three temples dedicated to Athena. In the foreground can be seen the remains of the first—built of stone in the seventh century and one of the earliest temple plans and columns preserved to us—and the remains of the second, a reconstruction dating from the sixth century. Beyond these ruins can be seen the foundations of two rectangular treasuries, and a tholos, or round building. Not visible in the photograph are the remains of a later Temple of Athena Pronaea, constructed during the fourth century B.C. The Sanctuary of Athena Pronaea includes the old temples, the two treasuries, the tholos, the new temple, and priests' quarters located beyond. Mycenaean sherds and idols have been found in the Athena precinct.

39 A section of the east frieze from the Siphnian Treasury. The east frieze depicts two scenes from the *Iliad:* the council of the gods on Mount Olympus and the battle for possession of the body of Achilles' friend, Patroclus. This particular section is from the latter; their shields raised and spears brandished, Agamemnon rushes forward behind Menelaus to attack the Trojans Hector and Aeneas. The Siphnian Treasury, Ionic in style, was built with the money produced from the gold mines of Siphnos to house the tithes that the Siphnians dedicated to Apollo annually. (530–525 B.C. Parian marble. Delphi Museum.)

40 In the foreground, the rocks of the Sanctuary of Ge (the Earth), the earliest sacred spot within what became the Sanctuary of Apollo; it was held sacred at least as early as the fourteenth century B.C., and referred to as "rocky Pytho" in the eighth century. In back is the Athenian Treasury, dedicated by the Athenians in the Sanctuary of Apollo after the establishment of the Athenian democracy in 507 B.C. The building was completely reconstructed with the original blocks (as far as was possible) between 1903 and 1906. The treasury, like the later Temple of Isis on Delos (see plate 33), is Doric, distyle-in-antis (two columns standing in between the terminating ends of the cella walls). The building was originally decorated with thirty relief panels (metopes), exhibiting the exploits of Heracles and the personal hero of Athens, Theseus. (507 B.C. Made of island marble. Delphi.)

41 A fragmentary pedimental sculptural group from the Temple of Apollo at Delphi. A lion attacks a deer, who arches his head around to look at his attacker. The square holes visible in the deer's head once held antlers. There was a series of temples dedicated to Apollo at Delphi. The first is known only from Homer; the second, dating from the first half of the sixth century B.C., was destroyed by fire in 548 B.C. These pedimental sculptures belong to the third temple, begun soon after, known as the Alcmaeonid Temple. Apollo, with a four-horse chariot (quadriga) was probably portrayed on the east front. Facing forward, he was flanked on either side by standing figures; two groups of lions attacking animals, of which this is one, were placed in each corner. (507 B.C. Parian marble. Delphi Museum.)

42 The oracular Temple of Apollo at Delphi, above the polygonal wall and the remains of the portico of the Athenians (see next plate). This temple, the most sacred area in Delphi, was one of the most renowned pagan sanctuaries. To it came pilgrims from all over the ancient world: gods and heroes, emperors and slaves. The temple is perilously situated beneath the Phoedriades ("the shining ones"), the twin peaks of Mount Parnassus; it was said that envious Poseidon took advantage of this fact, destroying the third temple, the Alcmaeonid Temple, with a landslide in 373 B.C. The rebuilding of the fourth-century temple (the present one) lagged for some forty years. It was patterned on the Alcmaeonid plan.

Through Pausanias we know that the pediments of the fourth-century temple were decorated with figures of Artemis, Leto, Apollo, the Muses, the setting sun, and with statues of Apollo's brother Dionysus, and his followers, the Thyiades. There were six columns across the front and the back (hexastyle) and fifteen along each flank. The longer flank proportions were due to an *adyton,* an underground room placed between the cella and the rear room (the *opisthodomos*).

The *manteion* (the oracular room), located in the temple, contained, according to Pausanias, a golden statue of Apollo and the tripod upon which the Pythia sat when she gave her prophecies; the Omphalos, a sacred stone supposedly having fallen from heaven and marking the centre of the earth, was excavated from this area.

43 Looking down towards the Treasury of the Athenians along the Sacred Way at Delphi, one comes to a circular area, the Alos. Grey stone benches, of which several remain, once encircled the area. Here the sacred drama representing Apollo killing the dragon, Python, was presented during the Pythian festival, held at first every eight, then every four years. To the right, four columns are all that remain of the portico of the Athenians, which was erected shortly after 478 B.C. to shelter the trophies won probably from the Persian emperor Xerxes. The architect of this portico used the archaic polygonal terrace wall (constructed as a retaining wall for the Alcmaeonid Temple of Apollo above) as a backdrop for his Ionic portico. The eight hundred inscriptions on the wall's polygonal stones are all official acts; many proclaim the freeing of slaves and date from about 200 B.C. to A.D. 100. Behind and to the left of the four standing columns are the broken remains of the column on which stood the famous statue of the sphinx dedicated by the Naxians. Immediately to the left (next to the Athenian Treasury) are the rocks of the Sanctuary of Ge. The Ionic capital and top drum in the left foreground originally helped to support the entablature of the stoa and marks the site of the seventh-century treasury dedicated to Apollo by the citizens of Corinth. This fabulously rich treasury, of which virtually nothing remains, was the most ancient structure of its kind. Herodotus attributed its construction to the tyrant Cypselus (657–627 B.C.), and enumerates the lavish treasure given by Gyges, Midas, and Croesus.

44 The Temple of Apollo at Delphi. The façade of the great oracular temple is preceded by an altar, which was presented by the Greeks of the island of Chios in gratitude for their liberation from Persian domination, in 494 B.C. or 479 B.C. The altar was constructed of a greyish black marble, in three degrees. Perhaps because of the temple's numerous destructions and rebuildings, many stories grew up about how Apollo built his temple at Delphi. Pausanias reports that the most ancient temple of Apollo was made of laurel; the second temple was made by bees from beeswax and feathers; the third was bronze. The fourth, made of stone, was apparently the actual temple that burned in 548 B.C.

45 "The Bronze Charioteer." Most of our knowledge of Greek sculpture comes from Roman copies and ancient literary sources. Rare is the original Greek marble statue or relief, rarer still the original bronze. Bronze was a valuable metal and could be melted down—often to make armour, coins, and even other statues. Therefore, the very few Greek bronze statues spared destruction—such as the charioteer—have been preserved by chance or unusual phenomena. He was knocked down in antiquity by an earthquake and, because he was the sacred property of the god Apollo, given a careful burial behind a terrace wall. Polyzalos, the Syracusan prince who commissioned the charioteer and his horses to commemorate a victory in the races at the Pythian games in 478 or 474 B.C., could scarcely have dreamed that his victory statue would become one of the most celebrated works in the history of art—and that his name and his deed would live on into eternity. The statue was probably the work of a south Italian artist. It was made in several pieces: even the eyelashes were added separately. The eyes were made with bone and semi-precious stone; the lips were outlined and set off with a thin strip of copper, and the fillet binding the head inlaid with silver. (470 B.C. Delphi Museum.)

46 The "Acanthus Column" at Delphi. This column was apparently a commemorative monument. Created towards the beginning of the fourth century, it was probably knocked down in the earthquake of 373 B.C. that destroyed the Alcmaeonid Temple of Apollo. The entire monument consisted of a column shaft of five drums (not shown); the capital is composed of three large acanthus leaves, which supported the three legs of a bronze tripod, now missing. The three dancers, or caryatids, were placed between the tripod legs. These maidens probably represent votaries of Apollo's sister, Artemis, executing the sacred dance performed in her honour at Caryae. (400–390 B.C. Parian marble. Delphi Museum.)

47 A general view of the sacred precinct of Delphi, looking down from the fourth-century B.C. theatre (restored in 159 B.C. and again during the Roman period). Directly beyond the theatre is the Temple of Apollo, and beyond Apollo's sanctuary is the Gymnasium terrace, with its circular swimming pool, and then the Marmaria. At the foot of the mountain to the left is the road to Arachova; above, off the road, is the crevasse containing the spring of Kastalia.

48 The Temple of Apollo at Corinth. The area of Corinth has been inhabited since the fifth millennium B.C. The gods blessed this part of Greece with fertile soil (the original word for Corinthian grapes, "Corinths," was later slurred to "currants"); with springs, one of which the winged horse Pegasus was said to have created by pawing the ground with his hoof; and with very fine clays (her ceramic industry brought Corinth fame and wealth). Her geographical position, commanding the isthmus, gave her a strategic pre-eminence over other cities. During the eighth century B.C. she began to form a vast commercial and trading empire, including Sicily, Italy, Greece, and Asia Minor. She became the city of luxury par excellence, and her brothels were infamous. Her wealth excited Roman greed, and in 146 B.C., on the pretext that she had betrayed Rome, the Roman general Lucius Mummius razed Corinth to the ground; her art treasures and statues were carted off to Rome and sold at auction. The ruins one visits today are not Greek but Roman. The Temple of Apollo escaped the wrath of Rome; it alone bears witness to the splendour of the old Greek city. In fact, although it stands on an earlier seventh-century sanctuary, the temple itself is one of the earliest preserved to us, dating from c. 640 B.C. It is Doric, similar in design to the Temple of Apollo at Delphi.

The shafts of the columns were not made up of drums, but are monoliths. In the centre foreground can be seen the Fountain of Glauke, cut out of natural rock. Glauke was Jason's second wife; she was killed by Medea, his first wife, who sent her a poisoned robe that burned her so painfully she cast herself into the fountain to ease the pain.

49 Arcadia, on the road to Bassae. Not far from here rises Mount Lycaeus. According to Arcadian legend, it was on this mountain (and not on Mount Ida in Crete) that Rhea secretly gave birth to Zeus.

50 and **51** The Temple of Apollo Epikourios (the succourer) at Bassae on Mount Kotilios near Phigalia. From the twilight years of the pagan world until A.D. 1765 this wonderfully preserved temple, designed by Ictinus, the architect of the Parthenon, was totally forgotten by man, isolated in the wilds of Arcadia. Pausanias said: "Of all the temples in the Peloponnesus, this one might be looked upon, after the one in Tegea, as the most admirable for the beauty of its stone and on account of its harmony."

The present temple replaces an earlier one dating from around 659 B.C. Ictinus probably designed this temple around 450 B.C., but before he could finish it, he may have been summoned by Phidias to Athens to design the most beautiful of all Doric temples, the Parthenon. The temple at Bassae is believed to have been finished shortly after 425 B.C. It also has six columns at the front and back and fifteen along the flank. A second room, the adyton, behind the cella, gives the temple its unusually long proportions.

The temple, like the Hephaisteion and the Parthenon, was not an orthodox Doric temple. Doric columns were placed peripterally on the exterior. The cella is sunken, and Ionic semicolumns are attached to the cella walls by means of spur walls (perhaps in imitation of the Heraion at Olympia). Above these columns was placed an Ionic entablature with a continuous Ionic frieze (now in the British Museum) representing the battles between the Amazons and the Greeks, and the Centaurs and the Lapiths (see also note 60). In addition, six metopes were sculpted above each of the Doric porches in a manner similar to that of the Temple of Zeus at Olympia. The metopes were not continued around the building as in the Parthenon. Originally the pediments were decorated with sculpture, now lost.

Unique to this temple are the southern columns' Corinthian capitals; between them stood an isolated Corinthian column—the earliest of its type—now disappeared. Although there is no proof, it may have represented an aniconic cult image of Apollo, much as the isolated Minoan columns on an altar may have symbolized the great Earth Mother. Another unusual feature is a door in the eastern flank of the building; perhaps the rising sun penetrated the inner rooms, illuminating the statue of the sun god Apollo.

III

ZEUS
OLYMPIA

I will sing of Zeus, chiefest among the gods and greatest, all-seeing, the lord of all,
the fulfiller who whispers words of wisdom to Themis as she sits leaning towards him.
Be gracious, all-seeing, son of Cronos, most excellent and great!
— *To the Son of Cronos, Most High* (Homeric Hymn XXIII)

According to myth, there were twelve Titans and Titanesses, and out of this number three Titanesses each took a brother to be also husband. This is how Rhea married her brother Kronos. Kronos had been warned by his mother, the earth goddess Gaea, and by his father, the starry sky, Ouranos, that one of his sons would overthrow him and rule in his stead. To prevent this prophecy from being fulfilled, Kronos took the precaution of swallowing his children alive as they were delivered from their mother's womb.

Rhea was inconsolable, and when her sixth child was about to be born, she prayed to her mother, the earth, and her father, the sky. They advised her to appear to give this child to her husband as Kronos demanded; in reality, she surrendered a stone wrapped in swaddling clothes. Kronos seized the stone and gulped it down, not realizing the ruse. The offspring, Zeus, was spirited off to Mount Ida (or Mount Dictae, or Mount Lyktos on Crete). There he was brought up by the nymphs Melissa (the name means "bee"), who fed him honeycombs, and Adrastia, who gave him milk from the goat Amalthea.

In gratitude, Zeus placed Amalthea among the stars, but first he took her skin, which was invulnerable, and made a protective aegis for himself. To the nymphs he gave one of Amalthea's horns, bestowing on it the remarkable property of continually refilling itself with whatever food or drink was desired—thus, Amalthea's horn became known as the cornucopia, the horn of plenty.

When Zeus attained manhood, he vowed to punish his father, Kronos. He forthwith summoned Metis, the goddess of counsel or wisdom, to help him. She gave Kronos a potion, so that he disgorged the five children he had swallowed, thus miraculously giving rebirth, as it were, to Hera, Demeter, Hestia, Hades, and Poseidon. These, along with Zeus's children Hephaestus, Hermes, Ares, Apollo, Athena, and Artemis, formed the hierarchy of the Olympian gods. Kronos, the titan, was then cast into Tartarus.

As a witness to his victory, Zeus placed the stone which Kronos had swallowed, believing it to be Zeus, at the foot of Mount Parnassus, supposedly in the sanctuary of Neoptolemos, at Delphi.

Hardly had the reign of the Olympian gods begun when the Titans, embittered over their fallen state, revolted. However, Zeus was victorious, with the help of the hundred-armed giants (the Hecatoncheires) and the one-eyed giants (the Cyclops), who had bestowed on him the gift of thunder and lightning.

This revolt had scarcely been subdued when the Typhons, another group of giants, possessed of enormous strength and legs which ended in serpents, rebelled. In order to attack the gods on Mount Olympus, these giants piled Mount Ossa on top of Mount Pelion; one giant armed himself with ice from Mount Athos, and another with Mount Oeta itself. Some of the giants were killed, and in order to subdue and imprison the rest, mountains and islands were piled atop their bodies. Athena buried Encelados under the island of Sicily; even to this day, when the giant moves, the entire island quakes. Eventually, order was established and Zeus assumed supremacy over all the gods.

Before his official marriage to his sister Hera, Zeus had been married several times. First he had married Metis, goddess of counsel or wisdom; next Themis, goddess of law and physical order; then Mnemosyne, goddess of memory, with whom he passed nine nights. (From these nocturnal visits were born the nine Muses.)

Zeus also fell in love with another sister, Demeter. When she attempted to stay his advances, he changed himself into a bull and violated her. Persephone was born from this holy union. After this, Zeus married Hera. Some legends say the marriage was consummated on Mount Cithaeron, others in the region of the Hesperides, and still others state that the first holy encounter took place at Knossos on Crete.

Pausanias tells the story slightly differently. He says that Zeus, in order not to arouse Hera's suspicions of his amorous intentions, came to her in the form of a cuckoo. It was winter, and the poor bird seemed to be trembling with the cold. The sensitive goddess was overwhelmed with pity for the frozen bird, and warmed it by holding it to her breast. Zeus then appeared in his natural form and tried to seduce the young goddess, but "ox-eyed" Hera was wary and wise, and succumbed only after Zeus had given her his solemn promise to marry her. From that time on, the cuckoo was sacred to the goddess Hera. "White-armed" Hera, to hold the attention of her philandering husband, took great pains to maintain her charms and desirability. Among other treatments, she bathed annually in the spring of Kanathos to restore her virginity.

The genitive form of Zeus's name, Dios, may be found in the root of the Sanskrit word "dyaus" and the Latin word "dies," both meaning "day." Originally, therefore, Zeus seems to have been a god of the sky and atmospheric phenomena—winds, clouds, rain, thunder, and lightning; thus he was originally associated with, or worshipped on, mountaintops.

Zeus, the supreme god, was omnipotent and omniscient. He was the source of all divination; he could give prophecies in person, through the rustling of oak leaves as at Dodona, or through an intermediary, such as the god Apollo, at Delos and Delphi.

According to Homer, Zeus possessed two jars: one contained blessings, the other misfortunes. From these he dispensed both to human beings, regardless of their individual merit. The person who received only misery was to be despised by gods and men alike—but Zeus could on occasion be just, kind, and compassionate.

The site of Olympia, the primary Panhellenic sanctuary of Zeus, lies between two gentle rivers, the Alpheus and the Cladeus, and nestles in a forest of fragrant pine trees. It contrasts vividly with the dramatic site of Delphi—but the air of tranquillity and sanctity which pervades the Altis is similar. Related, too, is its religious history. The original divinity revered here was not Zeus but the great Earth Mother Gaea. Her worship was ultimately supplanted by that of Zeus and his wife Hera, but she always retained an altar in the Altis and a festival was celebrated in her and Kronos's honour.

Recorded history at Olympia began in 776 B.C., the year the first Olympic games were held. The games, which were probably founded by the neighbouring town of Pisa, took place every four years in honour of the supreme deity, Zeus. This four-year period was called an Olympiad, and the Greek historians would often recount that an event happened, for example, in the first year of the fortieth Olympiad (i.e., c. 616/615 B.C.) The games were held during a five-day period, falling always during the period of the full moon some time between the end of June and the beginning of September. During this five-day span, a sacred truce was respected throughout the whole of Greece. All hostilities ceased, and woe to those who broke this truce.

The games began with sacrifices and libations to Olympian Zeus. Offerings were also made to Zeus the Fly Chaser (flies bring disease, and Zeus was the averter of disease), to Hestia, goddess of the hearth, and on the tomb of Pelops. All the athletes participating in the games swore on the altar of Zeus Horkios, in the *Bouleuterion*, or council house, to obey and uphold the rules of the games. Among the thirteen to fifteen various competitions were foot races, discus and javelin throwing, boxing and wrestling, and chariot racing. The victor was proclaimed by a herald after each contest. On the last day of the games, the winning athletes were crowned with olive leaves and received their prizes. The games were closed with a procession and a solemn banquet.

The Altis was exclusively reserved for the altars and temples of the gods. The administrative buildings were located elsewhere. Olympia, like the sanctuary of Apollo at Delphi, was governed by a body of magistrates and priests, each of whom had special duties. These officials and priests were usually chosen from local Elian aristocracy, and it was they who received the gifts and administered the revenues donated to invoke Zeus's aid and support.

The Olympic games were held continuously every four years for over ten centuries, until the edict of Theodosius I forbade the celebration of pagan festivals. The last Olympic games were held in A.D. 393, bringing to an end a long and glorious tradition.

In A.D. 426 Theodosius II ordered all pagan temples destroyed, and even the great Temple of Zeus at Olympia did not escape this desecration.

During the middle of the sixth century A.D., an earthquake knocked down what was left of the temple. A Byzantine village grew up in the sacred Altis, and a church was erected on the spot where the workshop of

Phidias had been located. Perhaps to spare the memory of the Olympian gods from further humiliation, the river Cladeus broke its ancient dykes, flooding the area and burying the sacred ruins beneath sand. During the seventh century the Slavs and then the Franks dared to establish a village in the Altis. Again Cladeus flooded the area, this time covering it with gravel. Zeus sent torrential rains that carried dirt and sand down from Mount Kronion, and Alpheus extended his meanderings. Soon proud Olympia with her holy altars and temples was safely interred under a protective covering of earth.

NOTES ON THE ILLUSTRATIONS

52 "Zeus," from a porous limestone pediment depicting the deification of Heracles. The building it decorated has not been identified. The father of many of the gods is seated on his throne; beside him (not shown) is his wife Hera, and a much smaller Heracles is being introduced to their divine majesties by his sponsor, the goddess Athena.

The limestone sculptures were originally painted. One must envision Zeus's face vividly colored; his Olympian beard blue, his large imperious eyes black, and the patterned embroidery of his garments in gay reds and yellows, with highlights of brown and black. (c. 550 B.C. Acropolis Museum, Athens.)

53 The River Alpheus, at Olympia in Elis. Myth tells us that Arethusa was a beautiful nymph from Elis and a follower of Artemis, goddess of the chase. One day, hot and tired from the hunt, she stopped to bathe in the cool waters of the Alpheus. The river god, seeing her exquisite body, fell passionately in love with her. She fled from him, but the god pursued. In distress Arethusa prayed to Artemis, who hid her in the ground and let her gush forth in the form of a fountain at Syracuse, Sicily. But Alpheus was not to be deterred. He followed her under the sea to Sicily, and there he finally mingled his waters with those of his beloved. The Alpheus river does, in fact, run underground in certain places.

54 The remains of the Temple of Hera in the Altis at Olympia. Although Pausanias says that the first Heraion was founded eight years after the Dorian invasions (the dates of the Dorian invasions are debatable, varying between 1200–1100 B.C.), any of these resulting dates are impossible; it probably dates from the end of the eighth century B.C.

The second temple, shown here, dates from the early sixth century B.C. Originally it was dedicated to Zeus and Hera together, but after the completion of the temple of Zeus, to Hera alone. The temple had six columns along its façade and back (hexastyle), and sixteen columns were placed along each side, thus forming a free-standing colonnade around the exterior of the cella walls (peripteral). Only the foundations and orthostates are of stone. The upper walls were made of sun-dried brick. This temple is unique because its columns are of different diameters, and its capitals are different in profile. Some columns are constructed of drums and others are monoliths.

The columns date from shortly after the building itself was erected through the Roman period. Of the two shown here, the column to the right dates from the sixth century; the other probably dates from the fourth century B.C. The original columns were made of oak, and when one rotted or was damaged, it was replaced in the style and proportions of its day. Pausanias saw one original oak column still standing in the opisthodomos when he visited Olympia in A.D. 173. At this moment the temple of Hera also served as a museum, and he saw and described many works of art. Among them was Praxiteles' famous statue of Hermes carrying the infant god Dionysus, which was found by German excavators in the very place Pausanias had recorded it to be some 1700 years earlier.

55 A column and drum—and, leaning against the drum, a Doric capital—from the Temple of Hera at Olympia. The Greeks usually cut stone columns in drums; the sections were held in place by metal dowels fastened through holes cut in the centre of the drums (as is visible here). They cut the flutes after the columns were in place.

56 Sculptures from the east pediment of the Temple of Zeus in the Altis at Olympia. The temple of Zeus has provided the largest ensemble of Early Classical sculpture preserved to us. The Early Classical period, one of the first conscious revolutions in the history of art, represents a radical return to simplicity of form after the rich decorative patterns of the Archaic period.

These sculptures depict the preparation for the fateful chariot race of Pelops and Oenomaus. Oenomaus, the son of the war god Ares, was King of Elis (near Olympia). He had one beautiful daughter, Hippodamia, and it had been prophesied by an oracle that Oenomaus would be killed by his future son-in-law. In order to prevent this, Oenomaus established a contest and let it be known that whoever could defeat him in a chariot race would win his daughter's hand in marriage, and half his kingdom—but, if he were the victor, the would-be suitor would forfeit his life.

Pelops, the son of King Tantalus of Phrygia, heard of the beauty of Hippodamia and of the generous prize, and he sought to try his luck. Unbeknown to the young man, thirteen before him had tried their luck and failed, for Oenomaus possessed wondrous horses, fleet as the wind, which his father, Ares, had given him. Pelops, however, did not leave the decision to fate but resorted to cunning and to treachery. He bribed Oenomaus's charioteer, Myrtilus, to loosen the pins holding the king's chariot wheels and to replace them with pins of wax. These, heated during the race, would melt and cause the wheels to come loose. As it happened, Oenomaus was thrown from his chariot and Pelops won the contest. Pelops dispatched Oenomaus with his lance, and won Hippodamia and the kingdom of Elis. He also killed Myrtilus, lest there remain any embarrassing witnesses.

This was Pelops's undoing, for Myrtilus was the son of Hermes. The god avenged his son by laying his curse on Pelops, the founder of Mycenae, and all his descendants. The curse manifested itself most prominently on Pelops's children, Atreus and Thyestes, and his grandchild Agamemnon. Only after Orestes, having killed his mother, Clytemnestra, had at last been purified by Apollo at Delphi, was the curse ended.

Pausanias visited Olympia in A.D. 173 and described the east pediment in the following manner: "There is, not yet begun, the chariot race between Pelops and Oenomaus, and preparation for the actual race is being made by both. An image of Zeus has been carved in about the middle of the pediment; on the right of Zeus is Oenomaus with a helmet on his head, and by him Sterope his wife, who was one of the daughters of Atlas. Myrtilus too, the charioteer of Oenomaus, sits in front of the horses, which are four in number. After him are two men. They have no names but they too must be under orders from Oenomaus to attend to the horses. On the very edge lies Cladeus, the river which, in other ways also, the Elians honour most after the Alpheus. On the left from Zeus are Pelops, Hippodamia, the charioteer of Pelops, horses, and two men, who are apparently grooms of Pelops. Then the pediment narrows again, and in this part of it is represented the Alpheus."

The theme of the east pediment is most appropriate for Olympia: Zeus, to whom every athlete before participating in the Olympic contests offered sacrifice as he swore to uphold the rules of the game, stands silently as the impartial arbiter, warning that the rules of the game must be followed or terrible consequences will ensue. (468–457 B.C. Parian marble. Olympia Museum.)

57 Statues from the east pediment representing Sterope, daughter of Atlas and wife of Oenomaus, with her kneeling handmaiden, and the divine, invincible horses which were a gift from Oenomaus's father, Ares. The so-called serving maid is kneeling in the exact place which Pausanias in his description allotted to Oenomaus's charioteer, Myrtilus. Could it be that Pausanias mistook the clothing she wears for the long chiton usually worn by charioteers, and the closely tied hair for the style usually adopted by athletes? (468–456 B.C. Parian marble. Olympia Museum.)

58 "The Seer," a groom examining his toenails, and personification of the river Cladeus, from the east pediment. Pausanias describes two men who may be grooms behind the horses. This description would fit the young man who is examining his toenails, but certainly not the older man. The latter sits with his hand raised to his chin, a gesture used in Greek art to symbolize sorrow or foreboding. This bearded man has been identified as the household seer who foresees the treacherous outcome of the race and the dreadful curse that will descend on the house of Pelops.

The pudgy body and the flaccid flesh of the old man are realistically rendered. This figure is one of the first representations in Greek sculpture of old age, and provides striking evidence of Early Classical artists' discovery of nature, after the artificial stylization of the Archaic period. (458–457 B.C. Parian marble. Olympia Museum.)

59 Personification of the river Cladeus, from the east pediment. This personification, along with that of the Alpheus, locates the scene of the east pediment topographically at Olympia itself. Cladeus acts as an impartial, almost disinterested, onlooker; his face gives an impression of purity and innocence. His physical position is bold; while it conveniently conforms to the narrowing triangle terminating the pediment, it and the manner in which the drapery caressingly curls and winds about his body, now revealing, now concealing, is reminiscent of the lazy river itself as it twists and meanders gently through the Olympian countryside.

Cladeus was not always gentle; sometimes when aroused he could and would overflow his banks and flood the countryside—and it is to him and to Alpheus that we owe the preservation of the Olympian architectural sculptures, buried under sand and earth in the sixth and seventh centuries A.D.

60 Sculptures from the west pediment. The battle of the Lapiths and the Centaurs at the wedding of Pirithous. Pirithous, prince of the Lapiths, a tribe living in Thessaly, was the son of Dia and Zeus, who in the form of a horse had seduced her. Pirithous celebrated his marriage to Hippodamia (sometimes referred to as Deidamia, and not to be confused with Pelops's bride) on Mount Pelion. All the Olympian gods except Ares, god of war, and Eris, goddess of strife, were invited along with many distinguished Greek heroes, among them Pirithous's friend Theseus. Also invited was a friendly neighbouring tribe, the Centaurs, half-man, half-horse. During the wedding feast the Centaurs, who had never tasted wine before, became inflamed with the power of the wine god, Dionysus. Eurytion, a Centaur, attempted to rape Pirithous's bride. The other Centaurs, who were rather giddy by this time, followed suit, seizing the first maiden or youth they could find. Theseus, Pirithous, and Caneus rushed to defend the honour of the bride and the rest of the Lapith women. Blood was spilled on both sides, and from that time on the Lapiths and the Centaurs were mortal enemies. Thus the offended Ares and Eris avenged themselves.

The battle of the Centaurs and the Lapiths became a favourite theme in Greek art. It formed a subject of the frieze of the Temple of Apollo at Bassae, and was also used on the southern metopes of the Parthenon. In the centre of the pediment is Pirithous. Next to him, on one side, are Eurytion, who has seized Pirithous's bride, and Caneus defending Pirithous. On the other side is Theseus, defending himself against the Centaurs with an axe. One Centaur has seized a maiden, and another has seized a handsome youth.

Apollo stands in the center of these pediments; like Zeus he appears as a remote being, a silent arbiter, calm. Although his right arm is raised, he is not taking an active part in the struggle. It is as if he were invisible in the midst of the fray. He is represented as a young ephebus, his hair looped up over a fillet in the fashion of athletes. The sculptor is advanced in his observation of nature, for the distribution of weight in the body is accurate. Apollo's eyes are directed towards Theseus, about to liberate a Lapith woman from her abductor. The Lapith woman pushes the attacker's head with one hand, and tears at his beard with the other. The Centaur's mouth is slightly open, as if wincing in pain. As the tale of the east pediment was a warning to those who would break the rules of a contest, the subject of the west pediment admonishes against breaking the rules of hospitality. And even today the Greek word for "foreigner" also means "guest."

For the present the great masters of the Olympia pediments must remain unnamed. It has recently been proposed that the sculptors may have come from the same island as the marble, Paros, which had a famous and venerable tradition of working marble (cf. Siphnian Treasury, plates 29, 35, 39). The statues and groups may have first been roughly blocked in the Parian quarries, and then the sculptors, accompanying the marble, may have finished the works at Olympia. In composition and feeling the calm and static east pediment sharply contrasts with the violent physical action of the west pedi-

ment. It has in fact been suggested that monumental wall painting may have influenced the composition of the west pediment.

61 "Hippodamia," or Deidamia, the bride of Pirithous, from the west pediment. The sculpture depicts Hippodamia violently seized by the Centaur Eurytion, his fingers grasping her breast. Yet in the face itself there is no show of emotion, no concern; her heavy-lidded eyes (originally painted) seem calm and serene; it is as if she, like Apollo, were totally removed from her chaotic surroundings.

Hippodamia's hair is bound with a net secured by a fillet, and her peplos gracefully rests on her shoulder and breast. (468–457 B.C. Parian marble. Olympia Museum.)

62 A fallen Doric capital and column drums from the Temple of Zeus in the Altis at Olympia. One of the largest Doric temples ever erected in Greece, it was designed by the architect Libon of Elis and probably begun during the Olympic festival of 468 B.C. It was dedicated at the time of the festival in 456 B.C., a date fixed by the shield attached to the apex of the east pediment by the Spartans to celebrate their victory at Tanagra in 457 B.C.

Six columns were placed on the front and rear (hexastyle) and thirteen columns along the sides. It was constructed in a coarse local limestone (actual shells are visible in the stone), covered with a thin coat of white stucco, and then painted. The pedimental sculptures, the metopes of the inner porches, the simas, and the roof tiles were all executed in Parian, the finest Greek marble.

Gilded bronze Victories, by the sculptor Paeonius of Mende, adorned the apex of the pediments, and gilded bronze tripods were positioned at the angles. The interior of the cella was divided into a nave and two side aisles by two rows of seven Doric columns, one on either side, each supporting a second row of columns. The temple housed one of the Seven Wonders of the ancient world, the gold and ivory statue of Olympian Zeus by Phidias. Until recently it was uncertain whether Phidias had executed this statue before or after the famous Athena Parthenos. Recent excavations at Olympia have uncovered the very workshop in which Phidias fashioned the wondrous statue. Molds on which some of the gold sheets of the drapery of the statue were hammered have been discovered, as well as Phidias's personal drinking cup (skyphos), inscribed in Greek "I belong to Phidias". The style and the date of these objects prove that Zeus was carved after Athena.

According to Pausanias, the temple and the statue were offerings to Zeus from the spoils which the Elians seized when they conquered Pisa in the Peloponnesus:

"The god sits on a throne and he is made of gold

and ivory. On his head a garland lies which is a copy of olive shoots. In his right hand he carries Victory, which, like the statue, is of ivory and gold; she wears a ribbon and—on her head—a garland. In the left hand of the god is a sceptre, ornamented with every kind of metal, and the bird sitting on the sceptre is the eagle. The sandals of the god are of gold, as is his robe. On the robe are embroidered figures of animals and the flowers of the lily. The throne is adorned with gold and with jewels, to say nothing of ebony and ivory. Upon it are painted figures and wrought images. There are four Victories represented as dancing women, one at each foot of the throne, and two others at the base of each foot. On each of the two front feet are set the Theban children ravished by sphinxes, while under the sphinxes Apollo and Artemis are shooting down the children of Niobe."

Strabo says: "The greatest [of the offerings in the Temple of Zeus at Olympia] was the image of Zeus, which Phidias, the son of Charmides, made of ivory, and which is of such great size that, though the temple is indeed one of the largest, the artist seems to have failed to take into account the question of proportions; for although he represented the god as seated, he almost touches the peak of the roof, and thus gives the impression that, if he were to stand up straight, he would take the roof off the temple. . . . and they recount this tradition about Phidias:

when Panainos (his brother) asked him what model he intended to employ in making the image of Zeus, he replied that it was the model provided by Homer in the following lines of the *Iliad*: 'thus spoke the son of Kronos, and nodded his dark brow, and the ambrosial locks flowed down from the lord's immortal head, and he made great Olympus quake.' "

Fragments of a colossal marble copy of the Olympian Zeus were found in the Temple of Zeus at Cyrene.

63 Fallen column drums from the Temple of Zeus. Olympia, like many areas in Greece, was subject to the displeasure of the earth-shaking god, Poseidon. The temple was shaken several times in antiquity. A severe quake that took place in 175 B.C. damaged the temple so much that both its façades had to be dismantled and rebuilt, and three statues from the west pediment had to be replaced. The great statue of Zeus was cracked, and was repaired by Damophon of Messene (who had made the famous statue of the mother of the gods at Lykosoura). It was probably at this time that Antiochus IV, an archpersecutor of the Jews, placed behind the statue of Zeus the embroidered curtain removed from the famous temple of Jehovah in Jerusalem.

These columns were knocked down during the sixth-century A.D. earthquake—the tragic *coup de grâce* for the temple of Zeus.

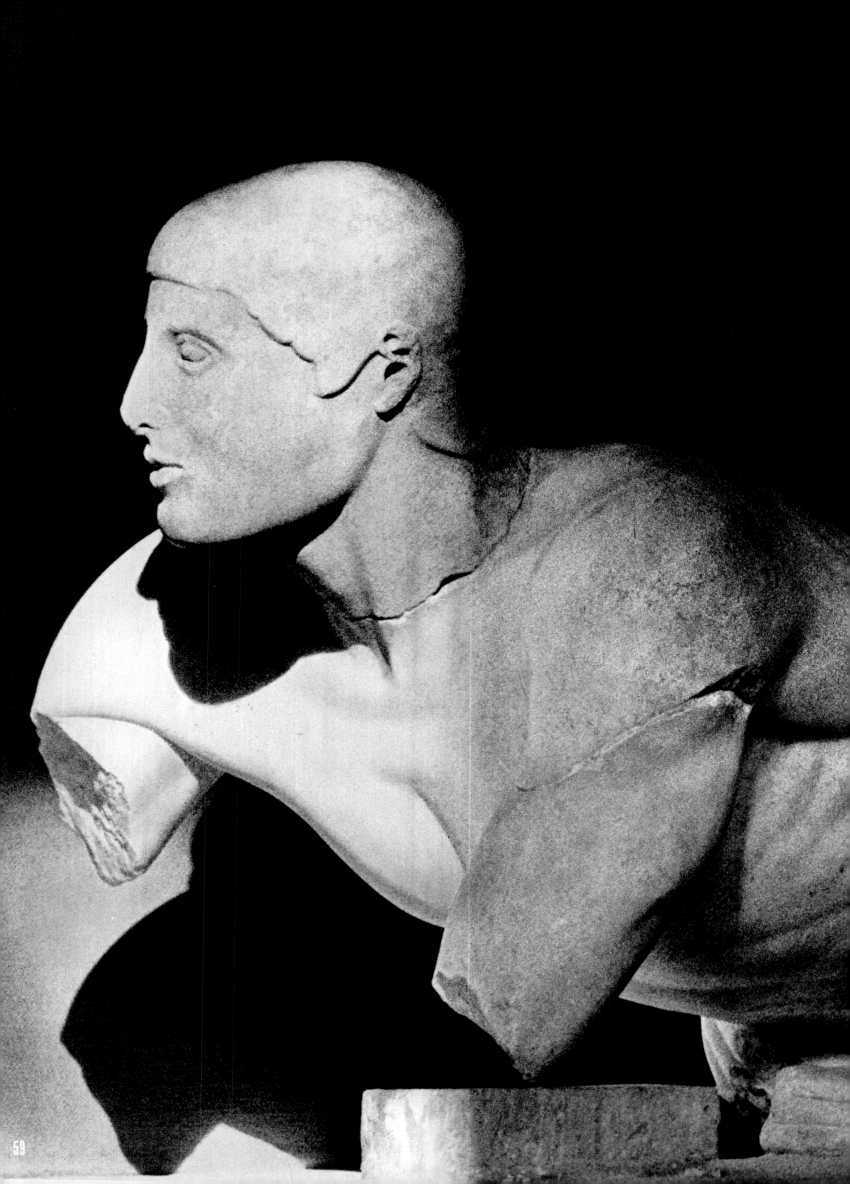

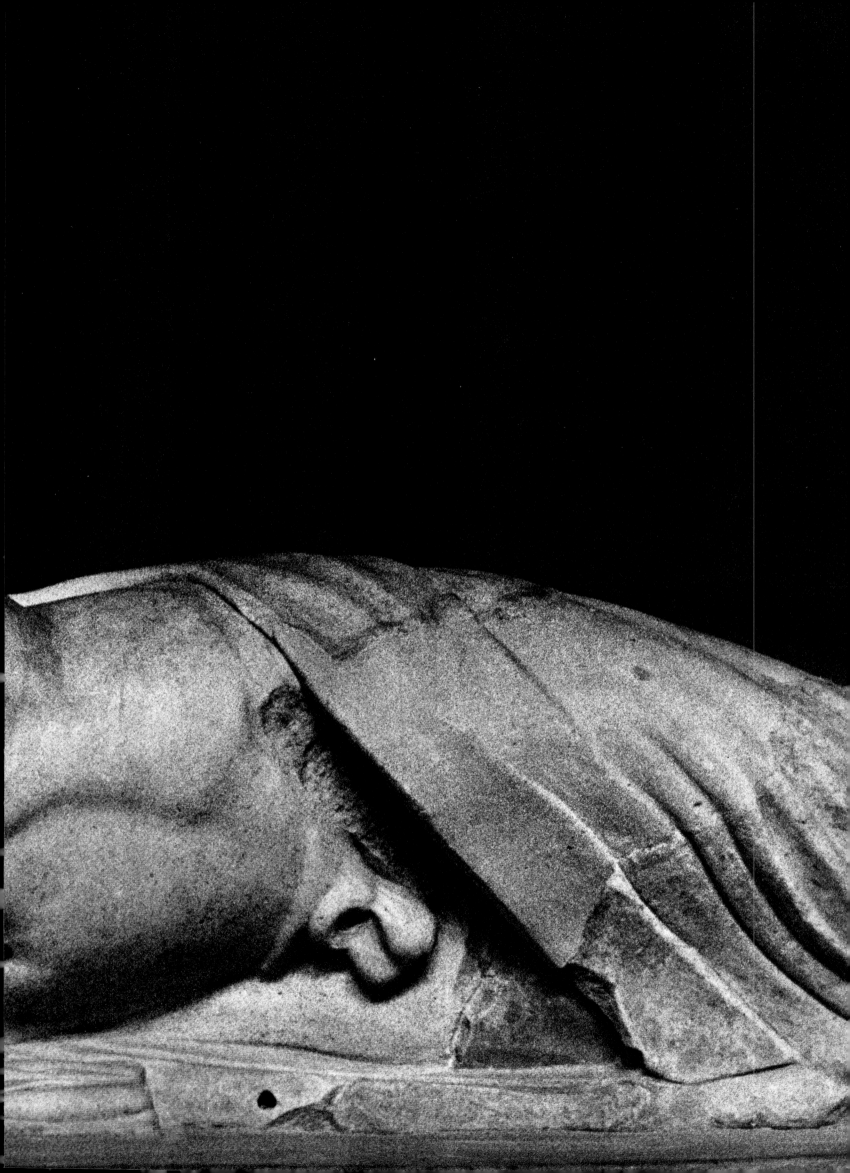

IV

ATHENA
ATHENS

I begin to sing of Pallas Athene, the glorious goddess, bright-eyed, inventive, unbending of heart, pure virgin, saviour of cities, courageous, Tritogeneia. From his awful head wise Zeus himself bare her arrayed in warlike arms of flashing gold, and awe seized all the gods as they gazed. But Athena sprang quickly from the immortal head and stood before Zeus who holds the aegis, shaking a sharp spear: great Olympus began to reel horribly at the might of the bright-eyed goddess, and earth round about cried fearfully, and the sea was moved and tossed with dark waves, while foam burst forth suddenly: the bright Son of Hyperion stopped his swift-footed horses a long while, until the maiden Pallas Athene had stripped the heavenly armour from her immortal shoulders. And wise Zeus was glad.

And so hail to you, daughter of Zeus who holds the aegis!
—*To Athena* (Homeric Hymn XXVIII)

According to myth, Zeus first married Metis, goddess of wise counsel, but then was warned that a child of Metis would become king of gods and men. Zeus therefore devoured his pregnant wife before this could take place.

Shortly afterwards Zeus began to suffer from a severe headache. Hephaestus—some say Prometheus—sought to help the god, and struck him on the forehead with a double-edged axe or hammer. To the astonishment of all, Pallas Athena sprang forth full-grown and in gleaming gold armour.

The word "Pallas" can take a masculine or feminine meaning, according to the way it is accented and inflected. It can mean strong man or strong virgin. Another myth attributed her epithet "Pallas" to a second father, Pallas, who attempted to violate his daughter; but Athena overcame him, flayed him, and wore the skin as her protective aegis. Yet another story tells of a third father, Brontes the Cyclops. Athena was also called Parthenos, "virgin."

One of the most important of Greek deities, Athena was invoked with Apollo and Zeus whenever solemn oaths were to be taken, for these three deities symbolized the embodiment of divine authority to all the Greeks.

Athena had a great variety of functions and attributes. As the virgin daughter of heaven, she was originally "the clear, transparent ether, whose purity is always breaking forth in unveiled brilliancy through the clouds that surround it." Like Zeus, she wore the aegis with the Gorgon's head, and was the mistress of thunder, lightning, and storms. But she was also the dew, supporter and protector of agriculture. Athena symbolized cleverness, wit, the moral and intellectual side of life, and, ultimately, in the Hellenistic period, wisdom. It was she who invented the flute and was the first to dance the Pyrrhic war dance. As Athena Ergane she presided over women's handicrafts, such as spinning and weaving; as Athena Hephaestaea she protected the art of smiths and metalworkers. She was goddess of forethought, Pronaea. She was said to have invented the plough and to have taught men how to yoke oxen, and she was associated with Poseidon as the inventor of horse-taming and shipbuilding. She was the goddess of war and strategy, and, as Athena Nike, the goddess of victory. As goddess of the pure air she gave health and warded off sickness. She was the patroness of social communities and of deliberative assemblies.

Athena was particularly revered in Attica. An Attic deity known as Erichthonius or Erechtheus, who represented the powers of the fruitful soil, was Athena's foster child. Three sacred services were performed at the opening of the ploughing season in Attica. One was in honour of Demeter, goddess of agriculture, and the other two honoured Athena, who had given Athens her livelihood, the olive tree.

Of all the goddesses Athena was considered the foremost protector of cities, and as such she was invoked as Polias or Polichos; but no city was dearer to her or honoured her more than the capital of Attica—the city which chose her name, and which she protected throughout Athens' long and brilliant history.

Of Pallas Athene, guardian of the city, I begin to sing. Dread is she, and with
Ares she loves deeds of war, the sack of cities and the shouting and the battle. It is she
who saves the people as they go out to war and come back.
Hail, goddess, and give us good fortune with happiness!
—*To Athena* (Homeric Hymn XI)

Legend states that King Cecrops, the first king of Athens, arrived on the Acropolis in 1581 B.C. Late Helladic I and II sherds (1600–1400 B.C.) have been found on the Acropolis in a house near the Erechtheion.

Athenian fortunes seemed to improve after the fall of Knossos, to judge from tomb furnishings, which began to include imported objects. The Athenian tombs have yielded Egyptian faïence and scarabs, Canaanite wine jars, tin, and liparite, which reveal expanded commercial ties with Asia Minor and Egypt, the Lipari Islands, and Spain. Apparently Athenian merchants of this late Mycenaean Age were more interested in overseas trade than commerce with the nearby Peloponnesus.

Around 1250 B.C., the gates and main fortification walls surrounding the Acropolis were constructed and a one-hundred-and-twenty-foot-deep shaft was dug to ensure a water supply. Mythology records that during the thirteenth century B.C., Mycenaean states were constantly attacking each other: the Peloponnesians versus the Athenians, the Athenians versus the Boeotians, the Athenians versus the Eleusinians.

As described in Chapter I, petty wars and internal struggles weakened the Mycenaean cities to the point where they apparently became easy prey to a stronger, more organized group—perhaps the Dorians and or the "sea peoples," possibly even helped by discontented and vengeful Mycenaeans. Athens was gracious and hospitable, and apparently received refugees from other Mycenaean sites. She alone of all Mycenaean cities escaped destruction; her people retired to safety behind the strong walls of the Acropolis.

The first great achievements in Greek art following the fall of the Mycenaean civilization were the ceramics and bronzes of the Protogeometric (1025–900 B.C.) and Geometric (900–700 B.C.) periods. Continuity between the art of the twelfth century and of this period is attested by pottery found at such sites as Knossos, Mycenae, Tiryns, Chios, Delos, Delphi, and Athens. But it was Athens that became the most important center of Geometric style, at least in pottery, and all the important artistic advances were made there. The cemetery at Athens outside the double gate (known as the Dipylon or Ceramicus because it was located near the potters' quarter) has produced a treasury of vases in sequence; most famous of all are the monumental Dipylon funerary vases.

Until the middle of the eighth century B.C., Geometric Greece was self-sufficient both economically and artistically. But then Greek cities such as Corinth and Athens again began to send out trading ships and merchants, and founded new colonies in Sicily and Italy and along the coasts of Asia Minor and the Black Sea. Vast new trading and commercial kingdoms were created.

This expansion once again brought Greece into contact with the venerable civilizations of Egypt and the Near East. New luxuries, such as delicately woven textiles and elaborately worked metal and ivory objects, were imported. These works, decorated with traditional Egyptian, Syrian, Hittite, and Assyrian motifs, began to influence Greek art, and although Greek artisans retained much that was inherently Greek in their work, they fell under the spell of the "exotic East" to such an extent that the era extending from 700 to 600 B.C. is called the Orientalizing period.

At the end of this period, around 600 B.C., Greece consisted of a number of powerful city-states, each possessing its own colonies. Each of these cities was an independent unit, proud of her own religious traditions and heroes, legal institutions, and individual artistic styles—but they were linked together by a common religion and a "consciousness of the same origins." Great sanctuaries, such as those at Delos, Delphi, and Olympia, formed the main religious bond. Pilgrims came to them from all over the Greek world to worship, to consult the oracles, and to compete in the sacred games. Non-Greeks, or "barbarians," were not permitted to take part in these Hellenic contests.

The Orientalizing period was followed by another brilliant era known as the Archaic period, dating from around 600 B.C. to the end of the Persian Wars, c. 480 B.C. During this period a change occurred in religious practices; although there are rare vestiges of temples dating from the end of the eighth century (the Heraion at Olympia, see plate 54), and a few from the seventh century (the Temple of Athena Pronaea at Delphi, see plate 38), it was during the Archaic period that temples sprang up all over Greece and monumental free-standing sculpture was born and developed, ultimately producing the great cult statues of the gods housed within the temples.

An extraordinary idea began to germinate in Athens towards the end of this period that eventually set Greece apart from the rest of the ancient world—a new idea of government, democracy. During the Geometric period and the seventh century, Greece was ruled by a few aristocratic families in a feudal system; during the latter part of the seventh century and the beginning of the sixth, these families were replaced by the rule of single men, who usually achieved power by championing the cause of the common people. They were known as the Tyrants.

In most cases the Tyrants were also the founders of their cities' greatness, as Pisistratus was in Athens. As the cities began to gain in prosperity, the arts too began to flourish. In Athens a number of temples and treasuries were built on the Acropolis. The few porous limestone pedimental sculptures from these temples preserved to us, such as "The Three Blue-Bearded Daimons" (plate 69), "The Lioness Attacking the Bull" (plate 68) and "The Water Carrier" (plate 70), suggest the beauty and gaiety of the early Acropolis. As Athens began to attain power and greatness under Pisistratus (561–527 B.C.), the fortunes of many of her families also grew, as is indicated by the numerous and splendid dedicatory offerings that adorned the Acropolis, such as the "Moscophoros" (plate 71), the many statues of maidens (*korai*), such as "The Peplos Kore" (plate 74) and "Kore 625" (plate 77), and those of riders (plate 83) and youths (*kouroi*), such as the "Critius Boy" (plate 80).

During the first quarter of the fifth century, Athenian development was hampered by the ever-present threat of Persia. Persia began her great expedition against Greece in 492 B.C., but Athens successfully defended the freedom of Greece three times, at the battles of Marathon in 490 B.C., Salamis in 480 B.C., and Plataea in 479 B.C. As a result, in the second quarter of the fifth century B.C., Greece began to recover and Athens emerged as her leading city-state. The great Temple of Zeus at Olympia was erected, and Phidias created his colossal statue of Athena Promachos. It was placed high on the Acropolis in such a position that sailors rounding Cape Sounion at Attica's southern tip (see plate 92) could see the reflection of the sun glinting on her helmet and spear—a reminder that the statue had been paid for "from the spoils of the Persians who had landed at Marathon."

With Pericles' rise to power in the second half of the fifth century, Athens reached the zenith of her glory. The cultural legacy left the world during this period is incalculable. As Athenian democracy was developing, Socrates was delivering his discourses in the streets, Aeschylus was ending his great career, and Sophocles and Euripides were brilliantly competing with each other. In 454–453 B.C. the treasury of the Delian League—the funds contributed by the Greek islands and city-states for the upkeep of the navy protecting them from Persia—had been transferred from Delos to Athens. Athens used the money to create temples and monuments to honour her gods and beautify her city. Painting and sculpture flourished, and the four masterpieces of Athenian architecture, so disparate yet so harmonious, rose on the Acropolis: The Doric Parthenon and Propylaea, and the Ionic Erechtheion and Temple of Athena Nike. Probably never again in the history of the West (unless in Renaissance Florence) was so much creative genius gathered in one place.

But Athens was not permitted to enjoy her supremacy for long. Sparta was jealous and in 431 B.C. the disastrous Peloponnesian Wars broke out, lasting until the Spartans' decisive victory at the battle of Aegospotami in 405 B.C. The Peloponnesian Wars were followed by internal bickering between the city-states; but soon a new power gathered force in the north under the leadership of Philip, King of Macedon.

Despite the eloquence of Demosthenes, Athens refused to heed his warnings, and Philip and his son, Alexander the Great, succeeded in subjugating Athens and eventually the whole of Greece. But this period of unrest also produced the three great sculptors of the fourth century, Praxiteles, Scopas, and Lysippus, as well as Plato and his pupil Aristotle. In the remarkably brief period of thirteen years, Alexander subdued all Greece, Egypt, and Asia Minor, extending his dominion to the Indus River in India. But he died before he was able to consolidate this vast empire, and it split up into a number of smaller kingdoms ruled by his former generals. Macedonia and Greece fell to Cassander, Thrace and Asia Minor to Lysimachus, the more Oriental provinces to Seleucus, and Egypt was governed by Ptolemy. There were also several independent states, such as Pergamon and Rhodes.

The Hellenistic Age, which commenced with the death of Alexander in 323 B.C. and terminated in 31 B.C. with the Battle of Actium, produced an art as different from Classical art as the latter had differed from art of the preceding centuries. Hellenistic artists attempted to explore all facets of man's character—not just his nobility and heroism. They depicted his banality and his exoticism, his brutality and generosity, his drunkenness and eroticism, in childhood and old age, in birth and in death. Gods became humanized, and humans were sometimes defied.

Ultimately, the emphasis on the individual and the independent spirit that was a part of Greece's genius was also to some extent her undoing. Unable ever to form a unified political entity, she was prey first to her own city-states and then to Rome, who annexed her, state by state, until in 31 B.C. all Greece was included in Rome's immense empire.

NOTES ON THE ILLUSTRATIONS

64 "Athena," on a metope from the temple of Zeus at Olympia, representing one of the twelve labours of Heracles, the cleaning of the Augean stables. Athena, Heracles's protector and patron goddess, stands beside him, lending him divine support. Heracles appears to be breaching the wall which will permit the Alpheus River to turn its course, thus allowing it to flow through and clean the filthy stables. The arrangement of metopes is unusual: there were only twelve, each one depicting one of the labours of Heracles. These sculptured metopes were not placed in their usual positions, that is, on the exterior of the temple, but in the interior, six on each short side of the exterior of the cella walls. (470–457 B.C. Parian marble. Olympia Museum.)

65 View of the north side of the Acropolis. The Parthenon, the temple of Athens' patron goddess, Athena, which now crowns the Acropolis, not only gives the impression of dwarfing the Erechtheion and the Propylaea, but of dominating all Athens.

Athens' royal Mycenaean palace was located on the north side of the Acropolis, partially under the present Erechtheion. The shape of the Acropolis as it is now was originally planned by Mycenaean architects and engineers. Mycenaean houses were built around the palace and clustered around the slopes of the Acropolis itself. The palace and the stronghold must have created an even more impressive sight in antiquity, springing abruptly out of its surrounding area. Perhaps the Acropolis's forbidding impression and seemingly impregnable rock walls that rose almost five hundred feet above the ground were the reason the Dorians never attacked the citadel itself.

66 The northwest area of the Acropolis, looking up from below Themistocles' walls towards the earlier fortification walls. Some of the original Cyclopean masonry is still visible in these walls, which were often repaired and remodelled. Above them stands the Erechtheion, of which the north porch and west side are visible here, and behind it the Parthenon, of which the north flank and the shorter western side can be seen. Nestled in the rocky area was the grotto of Aglauros (or Agraulos), a daughter of Cecrops, the legendary first king of Athens. Cecrops was believed to be an autochthonous, primordial being. His name means "earth born"; he had a human body that terminated in a serpent's tail. His wife bore him a son and three daughters. His daughters were named Agraulos (the dweller on tilled land), Herse (dewfall), and Pandrosos (the all-bedewed or all-bedewing). The last two seemingly were originally deities of the fertilizing dew and were later believed to give fruitfulness to the fields in Athena's service. Pan-

drosos was Athena's first priestess. She had a precinct of her own to the west of the present Erechtheion, which honours Erichthonius (or Erechtheus), the divine King of the Athenian Acropolis.

According to myth, Hephaestus demanded Athena's hand in marriage as payment for having assisted at her birth. She allowed herself to be led as far as the bridal bed—but when Hephaestus sought to consummate the marriage, Athena vanished, and his semen fell upon the earth. The earth goddess, Gaea, who was also called Chthonia, thereby gave birth to a child called Erichthonius and gave him to Pallas Athena, who in turn entrusted the child to the three daughters of King Cecrops. But virgin Athena had wanted to bring this child up in secret, unknown to the rest of the gods. She placed him in a round basket and forbade the daughters of Cecrops to open it. But they became curious, and when Agraulos and one of her sisters opened the basket they learned Athena's secret. What this secret was is debatable. Some say it was a serpent; others, a child guarded by one or two serpents; others, a child with serpent's feet. Whatever they saw drove the sisters insane, and they threw themselves off the Acropolis.

In Mycenaean times there was a secondary entrance to the citadel here, with stairs descending the precipitous slopes to the caves below. In 480 B.C., when the Persians invaded Attica, they were at first unable to take the Acropolis. Xerxes' soldiers then bombarded the Acropolis from the Areopagus with flaming arrows; then a few managed to scramble up these rocks through the grotto of Aglauros onto the Acropolis; they then opened the gates of the Propylaea and let the rest of the army enter the sacred precincts of Athena.

67 Looking through the Ionic columns of the Temple of Athena Nike (Athena bringer-of-victory) towards the west façade of the Parthenon on the Acropolis.

The low wall in the foreground is one of the rare remnants of the original Mycenaean fortification system. It once formed part of the double gate that guarded the main Mycenaean entrance to the Acropolis, citadel and royal palace. The entrance was protected by a huge tower and the double gate, which was the size of the Lion Gate at Mycenae (see plate 18). These walls and gates were probably built after 1250 B.C.

The southwest wing of the Propylaea was fitted against this Mycenaean wall, which in ancient times rose some forty-four feet above the pavement of the Propylaea. In antiquity one was never able to enjoy this particular view of the west façade of the Parthenon from the Temple of Athena Nike because it was obstructed by the south wing of the Propylaea, the temenos (sacred precinct) of Artemis Brauronia, and the precinct of Athena Ergane. The Sacred Way passed to the north of these temenoi along the north flank of the Parthenon. There are many cuttings in the virgin rock of the Acropolis where dedicatory stelae, votive offerings, and the variously gay and sober Archaic statues of youths and maidens had originally been placed before the Persians invaded, burned, and desecrated the Acropolis in 480 B.C.

68 A section from a porous limestone group that probably originally decorated the rear pediment of the Hecatompedon, an early predecessor of the Parthenon. The sculptures were found in the "porous layer" to the east and south of the Parthenon, and evidently belonged to the temple that was dismantled in order to build what became known as the "older Parthenon."

The sculptural group depicts a lioness slaying a young bull; originally it may have been balanced in the other half of the pediment by a similar group, or perhaps a single lion, without a victim, waiting for the lioness (represented here) to finish the kill. The narrowing angles of the pediments may have been filled with giant writhing snakes.

The motif of a lion slaying an animal, usually a bull or stag, originated in the Near East and had a long history in Greek art extending from Mycenaean times (see plate 41, the pedimental group of the Temple of Apollo at Delphi). During the Archaic period, and especially on the Athenian Acropolis, this theme was monumentalized, becoming the central subject of several temple pediments. Perhaps a deeper, more symbolic meaning lurks behind this venerable, seemingly decorative scheme.

The master who created this group has added great pathos to the scene. The lioness's nipples, which dispensed the life-giving fluid, are delicately draped over the neck and head of the dying bull, who gasps in the last throes of his mortal agony. But certain Archaic conventions contradict this graphic realism: the tufts of belly fur were executed in continuous, identically stylized patterns, while the eye of the bull was rendered with a cutting compass that created a design of concentric circles. These sculptures were originally painted with lively colours; remnants of the colours may be noted on the nipples and the eye of the bull. (570–550 B.C. Porous sculpture. Acropolis Museum, Athens.)

69 Three-winged, snake-tailed daimons, probably from the main pediment of the Hecatompedon. Because of the rather special colour of the beards of these three genial-looking creatures the pediment they decorated has been dubbed the "Bluebeard" pediment. The three monsters were balanced at their left by Heracles wrestling with Triton. Both groups

framed a central symmetrical composition of two lions slaying a single fallen bull.

Whom or what did these three daimons represent? They are winged and have bodies terminating in snake tails; therefore, they may be related to the terrifying Typhon, the creator of devastating hurricanes, or to Boreas, the North Wind; but their benign aspect suggests that they may represent the gentle cooling breezes. Their bodies, which are decoratively entwined in an elongated corkscrew effect, form a pleasing counterpart to Triton, while conforming to the narrowing angle of the pediment.

The depth of the relief is twenty-two inches. Fortunately, the original colour is preserved, which enlivens their seemingly expectant faces and twisted bodies, and gives one a vivid impression of how ancient painted sculpture must have looked. (470–550 B.C. Porous limestone. Acropolis Museum. Athens.)

70 "The Water Carrier" ("Hydrophore") from the so-called "Olive Tree" pediment. Some scholars identify the building from which the young maiden is emerging as the pre-Erechtheion, assuming that the tree appearing behind the garden wall (not shown here) is the sacred olive tree of Athena. Others, however, have suggested that the building is a fountain house, because the maiden emerging from it is wearing on the top of her head a round pad of cloth, which was used in antiquity (and it is to this day in Greece and the Middle and Far East) to cushion and balance objects carried on one's head, such as water pitchers (hydriae). The pedimental figure belonged to an unknown "Temple A," located somewhere on the Acropolis; the rear of this temple was decorated by a representation of the combat of Heracles and the Triton.

The depth of the relief is ten inches. "The Water Carrier" is an example of early Archaic sculpture. She has rather large ears that are flattened back against her patterned tresses. Her red peplos and green stole-like garment (himation) still retain some of their once bright colouring. (570–550 B.C. Porous sculpture. Acropolis Museum, Athens.)

71 "The Calf-bearer," or "Moscophoros," one of the earliest of the marble statues on the Acropolis. It was executed in the light greyish-blue marble of Mount Hymettus. An inscription, [R]ombos, on the base of the statue identifies it as a votive gift, in all probability representing the statue's dedicator himself, [R]ombos. Perhaps he is carrying the calf to sacrifice at the altar of one of the gods worshipped on the Acropolis. The motif—a man bringing a calf or a ram on his shoulder—had very early origins (see the Cretan bronze statuette, plate 14) and was perpetuated in Christian art.

Here [R]ombos is holding the legs across his chest

in a chiastic position. [R]ombos's eyes were inlaid with semiprecious stone and ivory or bone, which have long since disappeared, and his beard was originally painted like those in the "Bluebeard" pediment. The modelling of both faces was conceived in broad terms: superfluous details were eliminated, the hair was summarily rendered with a claw chisel. The lips are drawn up at the corners in the so-called "Archaic smile"—the ubiquitous convention of the Archaic period, used to enliven the face. (c. 570–550 B.C. Acropolis Museum, Athens.)

72 The Hephaisteion. This temple has long been the center of controversy concerning its identity and chronology. It was previously known as the Theseion because some of Theseus's adventures were represented on the metopes placed on the flanks; but the real sanctuary of Theseus, the legendary hero and founder of the Attic state, was located in a different area of the city.

The Hephaisteion is located below the Acropolis on a small hill slightly west of the Agora, or market place, near the potters' quarter, the Ceramicus, and the workshops of the metalworkers. Thus the temple was dedicated to the god of the forge, and to Athena Hephaistaea, as goddess of handicrafts. Their lost bronze cult statues were executed by Alcamenes between 421 and 415 B.C.

The Hephaisteion is the best-preserved example of the perfected Doric hexastyle temple. Ironically, this pagan temple owes its excellent preservation to its conversion into a Christian church dedicated to Saint George towards the beginning of the fifth century A.D.

It was begun in 449 B.C. and was the finest of the four temples probably designed by the unknown "Theseum" architect. The other temples were the Temple of Poseidon at Sounion, executed c. 444 B.C.; the Temple of Ares (which also contained a cult statue by Alcamenes), built about 440 B.C. but removed from its original site and rebuilt in the Agora in front of the Hephaisteion during the Augustan period around 14–10 B.C.; and the Temple of Nemesis at Rhamnus constructed around 436 B.C.

The Hephaisteion consists of a cella (the principal enclosed chamber), a *pronaos* (an open vestibule before the cella), and an *opisthodomos* (a back room). It is surrounded by a peristyle of six columns across the front and rear, and thirteen along each flank. As in the Parthenon, there was a double story of Doric columns in the interior of the cella. Although the temple is basically Doric, there are some Ionic elements, such as the continuous frieze placed above the Doric columns in the opisthodomos and the pronaos. Of the external metopes only eighteen were sculptured—ten along the east front representing the deeds of Heracles, and the four which joined the east end on the north and south flanks depicting

the exploits of Theseus. The pediments were also filled with sculpture, fragments of which have been found.

The Hephaisteion was distinguished by a singular feature: in antiquity (as now in imitation of its original setting) it was surrounded by a garden. There are cuttings in the rock and ground around the temple to contain flower pots. The temple was constructed of Pentelic marble, while the sculptures were executed in marble from Paros. (449–444 B.C.)

73 A sphinx from a grave monument. The word "sphinx" means "the throttler." She had a long history; originally Egyptian, she flourished in the Near East, entered Mycenaean art, and was eventually adopted by the later Greeks.

Perhaps the most famous sphinx in Greek mythology was the one that Hera (some say Ares or Dionysus) brought from Ethiopia and sent to Thebes in Boeotia. Perched on a huge rock near the city, she asked every passerby the famous riddle, "What walks on four legs in the morning, on two at noon, and on three in the evening?" Those who were unable to answer were then thrown from the rock and killed.

At last Oedipus guessed the correct answer: man. As a child, he crawls on four legs, in the morning of his life; as a man, in the noon of life, he walks erect on two legs; and in old age, the evening, he walks on three legs, one being a cane. The sphinx gave a horrible shriek and hurled herself from the rock.

Sphinxes were used as dedicatory offerings, such as the Naxian sphinx at Delphi; as acroterial figures, such as the statues that decorated the Siphnian Treasury; and as the finials of grave stelae or monuments. This sphinx was found in the cemetery of the Ceramicus, the main Athenian cemetery, whose graves date back in unbroken succession to the Mycenaean period. She has the body of a lion, the wings of a bird, and the head of a maiden. The sphinx was used as a guardian, an apotropaic creature to ward off evil. This sphinx seems to merge with the shadows of death, of the past, but she also seems to look rigidly and alertly into the future.

She suggests the symbol she came to represent in the minds of the ancients—the hope of rebirth and eternal life. (c. 550–540 B.C. Ceramicus Museum, Athens.)

74 "The Peplos Kore" (so named because she wears a Doric peplos) is the second of four superb works attributed to the Attic artist Phaidimos. She is probably the finest of all the korai figures preserved to us from the Acropolis. "The Peplos Kore" may be a votive statue representing an unknown aristocratic Athenian maiden who once participated in the sacred Panathenaic Festival, held every four years in Athena's honour.

"The Peplos Kore" bears a certain resemblance to the goddesses represented on the east frieze of the Siphnian Treasury at Delphi, especially around the eyes, ears, and mouth, and in the rendering of the crinkled locks of hair. But she is far more self-contained and restrained. Her somewhat protruding eyes were painted, as was her hair, and she wore a bronze wreath or diadem, and earrings dangled from her pierced ears. She may have held a wreath in her right hand, and carried a phiale in her left hand from which she would have poured a libation to Athena. (530–525 B.C. Parian marble. Acropolis Museum, Athens.)

75 The head of a horse, detail of a statue found on the Acropolis. Originally this formed part of a sculptural group, a horse and rider (now only the left leg and hand and part of the right leg of the rider are preserved; the horse has lost his right foreleg and both his rear legs).

There are three categories and series of votive dedications on the Acropolis: the maidens called korai, the youths called kouroi, and the horses and riders. These three groups are richly represented on the splendid frieze from the Parthenon depicting the Panathenaic procession. One may assume that, like the korai and kouroi groups, these young equestrians may depict scions of aristocratic families who once took part in the quadrennial celebrations.

With his head held alert and erect, his stylized curving mane, and the curved incised lines around his mouth, the horse too seems to be a dignified, aristocratic animal. (520 B.C. Parian marble. Acropolis Museum, Athens.)

76 The Acropolis seen from the hill of Philopappos. The Mycenaean entrance to the Acropolis was just south of the present Propylaea at the head of the ascent. The Temple of Athena Nike and the later monument of Agrippa are here dwarfed by the monumental entrance gateway to the Acropolis, the Propylaea, which was originally intended to cover the whole width of the Acropolis. The magnificent scheme designed by Mnesicles and begun in 437 B.C. unfortunately was first abridged, then interrupted by the outbreak of the Peloponnesian Wars in 432, and never finished. This must have sorely grieved the goddess Athena, for she was said to be very much involved with the work and eager for its completion. In his *Life of Pericles* Plutarch recounts that one of the most able of the workmen "slipped and fell from the height, and lay there in very poor condition, given up for dead by the doctors." Pericles was very despondent; Athena appeared to him in a dream and prescribed a course of therapy; when Pericles awakened he tried it and quickly and easily cured the man. As a result, he erected a bronze statue of Athena Hygieia on the Acropolis.

The Propylaea as it was constructed was composed of a central building that was flanked by a wing on either side of the western façade, giving it the appearance of a T-shaped plan. The central building consists of two Doric hexastyle porticos facing east and west. The eastern being on much higher ground, the interval between the two porticos was ingeniously bridged by three slender Ionic columns (which are proportionally taller than Doric columns) on either side of the central roadway. Parallel to the two porticos was the cross-wall, pierced by five doorways corresponding to the axes and widths of the various intercolumniations of the two façades. The central entrance was the widest.

The northwest wing (to the left here) was used as a picture gallery (pinakotheke) and outfitted with windows. When Pausanias visited the Acropolis this room was actually filled with paintings, which he described. On the south side (the right side) the wing which would have corresponded to the pinakotheke stopped short at the Mycenaean wall (see plate 67). The westward projection of this southern wing was cut because this area had previously been claimed for the future construction of the Temple of Athena Nike (see plate 88). The building was constructed of Pentelic marble. Bosses, used for lifting blocks, are still visible on many of the wall blocks. They attest to the unfinished state of the building, since once the blocks were in place the bosses were removed.

77 "Kore 675" (referring to its official inventory number in the Acropolis Museum, universally accepted by scholars) was probably executed by an island sculptor, perhaps from Chios, and as such is considered Ionic, as opposed to "The Peplos Kore" (plate 74), which is an example of Attic art. The kore is dressed in the Ionic chiton, a long chemise-like garment, over which is draped a himation, a mantle or cloak. The Ionic chiton was usually made of linen, imported from Egypt or the Near East, draped to form numerous soft, delicate folds. Here the maiden held her chiton with her left hand, which enabled the artist to add a profusion of intricate folds to the somewhat artificial patterns already created by the vertical and diagonal zigzagged folds. Her grasping of the drapery in this particular area of the body may also be an allusion to the age-old gesture of the fertility goddess, indicating her sex. The original colours are well preserved, and the painted patterns discernible on her himation and chiton suggest the kind of embroidered designs well-dressed maidens used as adornment. The kore's right arm originally may have held an offering or a phiale with which to pour a libation. (520 B.C. Parian marble. Acropolis Museum, Athens.)

78 The west façade of the Parthenon. The Parthe-

38

non was officially the temple of Athena Polias, but since there was another temple on the Acropolis (the Erechtheion) that bore that name, the Parthenon was first referred to as the Hecatompedon (the hundred-foot temple), a name inherited from its predecessor on this site. The name "Parthenon" (the chamber of the virgin) originally referred only to the west room, but a century later was applied to the whole building.

It was designed by two architects, Ictinus and Callicrates. Ictinus wrote a book about his masterpiece, now lost. The Parthenon was erected in the incredibly short span of nine years, between 447 and 438 B.C., at which time it and its fabulous cult statue of Athena were dedicated at the Panathenaic Festival. Work on its pedimental sculptures continued until 432 B.C., under the splendid direction of Phidias.

The Parthenon, built of Pentelic marble, is the largest Doric temple in Greece and the most imposing building on the Acropolis. For all its grandeur and monumentality, the building embodies the subtlest of aesthetic refinements. There is not one straight line in the structure. If there were, the eye would distort the vertical lines to appear to be bulging and the horizontals to be buckling. The architects took into consideration these human optical distortions and compensated for them by curving and tilting the columns, the stylobate, the walls, and the architraves so they would appear to be straight to our eyes.

There is a brilliant alternation of horizontals and verticals. The horizontal lines of the platform steps and stylobate are balanced by the vertical accents of the columns, which are in turn interrupted by the architrave; these are relieved by the vertical triglyphs, of which every other one is placed directly above a column. Then the vertical lines are fused with the horizontals in the gentle triangular pediment that caps and completes the ensemble.

The east and west pediments were decorated with some of the most superb and perfect sculpture the ancient world had yet witnessed. The Parthenon had remained almost intact, and the sculptures had survived *in situ* for more than 2100 years, until, unfortunately, the Turks used the building as a powder magazine. On September 26, 1687, Venetian forces commanded by Francesco Morosini bombarded the Acropolis, and a shell fell on the Parthenon, thus destroying most of the inner building with the exception of the opisthodomos and fourteen columns of the peristyle.

The birth of Athena was represented in the east pediment, which was the principal façade. The central group of statues, Athena, Zeus, and Hephaestus Prometheus, was destroyed *c.* A.D. 450, when the Parthenon was converted into a Christian church dedicated to another holy virgin, the Virgin Mary. Evidence suggests that Athena was portrayed as fully grown, armed, and springing to the right of an en-throned Zeus. A Victory flew towards Athena to crown her—while Hephaestus Prometheus, double-axe in hand, moved away in surprise to the left of Zeus.

The corner figures may be restored with certainty: first, the sun god Helios rose out of the sea; two heads of his four-horse team were seen. Then a man reclining on a panther skin (Dionysus or a personification of Mount Olympus, where Athena's birth took place); next Demeter and Persephone seated on chests. Then Iris or Hebe (the now disappeared central group) and the so-called Three Fates. In the extreme angle Selene, goddess of the moon, was shown sinking into the sea with her four-horse chariot. The positions and actions of Helios and Selene would seem to suggest symbolically that the time of Athena's birth was that uncertain hour which is neither day nor night, that moment which takes place only at the full moon, when the sun rises at the same instant that the moon sets.

The west pediment was devoted to the famous contest between Athena and Poseidon for the possession and patronage of the land of Attica and the city of Athens. King Cecrops was invited to judge the dispute. Poseidon struck the rock of the Acropolis with his trident, and caused the "sea"—a salt spring —to gush forth (the marks of his trident are to be seen in the north porch of the Erechtheion). Athena touched her spear to the ground, and an olive tree sprang up. Athena was victorious.

At the centre of the pediment the two divine contestants perform their miracles, flanked on either side by their two-horse chariots, two messengers of the gods, Hermes and Iris, and various other deities. In the northwest angle reclined a river god, Illissus or Cephissus; Pausanias compares this statue to the river gods shown on the Temple of Zeus at Olympia (see plate 59). The only two preserved torsos *in situ* perhaps represent Cecrops and one of his daughters.

The sculptures of the west pediment were left relatively intact by the explosion. But Morosini, the Venetian leader, apparently not content with the damage he had already wreaked on the Parthenon, subjected it to further destruction, albeit accidentally. He attempted to take down the figure of Poseidon and the horses of the central group. His tackle broke, and the sculptures were dashed to pieces. No attempt was made to rescue the fragments. Like innumerable other Greek marble masterpieces, they were burned in kilns to make lime used to whitewash houses, churches, and mosques.

The pediment may have depicted a clash between the deities of two races (such as Heracles' attempt to steal Apollo's tripod at Delphi—see plate 35), since Poseidon was first worshipped in Athens and then supplanted by Athena. The most artistically advanced of all the sculptures of the Parthenon, these figures were probably the last to be created, and may be dated between 438 and 432 B.C. Most of the pedimental sculptures are in the British Museum.

79 "Kore 686," dedicated by Euthydikos. This statue is the latest of the Archaic maidens, the last but one of the many votive korai on the Acropolis, and the most original. It has been suggested that the work may be Peloponnesian rather than Attic. She is the harbinger of the coming new style of the Early Classical period: the painted eyes are carefully framed by heavy lids; the charming Archaic smile is now replaced by a certain sobriety. The expression around her full sensuous lips has been interpreted as almost pouting, and so she is called "La Boudeuse"—"The Pouter."

The artificially stylized folds and diagonal zigzags of the drapery so dear to the Archaic artist have given way to smooth broad verticals or sweeping lines, which here provocatively accentuate the left breast while concealing the other. Both breasts are emphasized by her carefully placed tresses of hair. Her head is crowned by a simple hairband.

She looks out at the world with a seriousness that almost suggests a foreknowledge of the terrible holocaust that would soon consume the Acropolis. In 480 B.C. the Persians stormed the Acropolis, set fire to all its temples and shrines, and stole or destroyed all the votive offerings. When the Athenians returned to the Acropolis after their victory at Salamis, they salvaged what they could. They gathered and piously buried the broken sacred dedications on the Acropolis. It is ironic that the sculpture presented in plates 75, 77, 79, and 80 was preserved to us because of its sudden catastrophic destruction in antiquity by the Persian soldiers of Xerxes. (490–480 B.C. Parian marble. Acropolis Museum, Athens.)

80 "Kouros 698." Because of a certain stylistic resemblance to "The Tyrant Slayers," Harmodius and Aristogeiton, executed by the sculptors Critius and Nesiotes, this statue has been thought to be by the sculptor Critius and is called the "Critius Boy."

The kouros's eyes were originally inlaid with semiprecious stones and bone or ivory—similar in technique to that used in bronze-working (see "The Bronze Charioteer" from Delphi, plate 45) but rarely marble (but see also "Moscophoros," plate 71). His hair was bound up over a fillet. He is one of the earliest statues to stand on one leg while relaxing the other. The sculptor has successfully rendered the resulting shift in weight and in the axis of the body, as well as the interreaction of muscles, thus closely imitating nature. Heretofore the kouroi statues had been bound by a standard rigid pose, enlivened only by placing the left foot forward (see "Cleobis and Biton", plate 37), a convention Archaic artists had borrowed from Egyptian sculpture. (c. 485–480 B.C. Parian marble. Acropolis Museum, Athens.)

81 The interior of the Parthenon looking from the main chamber of the cella (the Neos Hecatompedos) towards the western room (the original Parthenon, or chamber of the virgin). The wall that originally separated the two chambers has disappeared. The present Parthenon was built over two earlier temples, which had also been dedicated to the virgin goddess Athena. The Hecatompedon, to which the porous lioness devouring the bull (plate 68) and the three blue-bearded daimons (plate 69) belonged, was the first; it may have been dedicated at the official establishment of the Panathenaic Festival in 566 B.C.

In 490 B.C. the Athenians won their singular dramatic victory over the Persians at Marathon. They apparently decided to demolish the porous Hecatompedon (as well as the Pisistratid Temple also dedicated to Athena) and to erect a grandiose temple, probably on the site of the Hecatompedon.

The marble quarries on nearby Mount Pentelicus had recently been opened, and the new temple was to be built of this material, thus initiating construction in marble on an imposing scale. But this temple was never finished; when the Persians burned and sacked the Acropolis in 480 B.C., they totally destroyed it. Known as the "Old Parthenon," it remained for more than thirty years a sacred war memorial. A number of its blocks and column drums were placed in the north wall of the Acropolis (see plate 65); the rest were recut for the present structure. The Parthenon was constructed with a peristyle consisting of eight columns (octastyle) on the front and rear and seventeen columns on either flank (a number of the peristyle columns have been restored and re-erected in modern times). Within this were placed six-columned (hexastyle) porticos at both ends. The cella contains two separate chambers: a rear chamber entered from the opisthodomos in which were placed four Ionic columns supporting the ceiling, and the cella of a hundred feet, or Neos Hecatompedos, a name inherited from the earlier Hecatompedon.

Originally there were ten Doric columns on either side of the Neos Hecatompedos and five columns across the rear, which carried an architrave with superimposed Doric columns above. This double-storied gallery formed an architectural frame for Phidias's famous gold and ivory statue of the goddess Athena. It also formed a type of ambulatory so that pilgrims might walk around the forty-foot-tall cult statue to view it from all sides. Although this magnificent cult statue has long since disappeared, ancient literary sources give us some idea of what it may have looked like.

Pausanias writes, ". . . in the temple which they call the Parthenon . . . the cult image itself is made of ivory and gold. In the middle of her helmet there is placed an image of a sphinx, and on each side of the helmet griffons are represented. . . . Griffons are beasts which look like lions, but have the wings and beak of an eagle. . . . The statue of Athena stands upright, and wears a tunic which reaches to the feet, and on her breast the head of Medusa, made of ivory, is represented. . . . In one hand she holds a figure of Victory about four cubits high [about eight feet] and in the other she holds a spear; at her feet is placed a shield, and near the shield is a serpent. This serpent would be Erichthonius. On the base the birth of Pandora is represented in relief. The poems of Hesiod and others tell how Pandora was the first woman."

Pliny describes the statue's shield: ". . . the battle of the Amazons is carved in a circular pattern on the convex side of her shield; likewise on the concave side of it he represented the struggle of the gods and giants, and on her sandals that of the Lapiths and Centaurs. . . ."

82 Looking from the exterior of the west façade of the Parthenon through the outer peristyle upwards at the interior hexastyle portico that precedes the rear chamber, the opisthodomos; the rear wall of the opisthodomos and a section of the virgin's chamber, the Parthenon, are visible in the background.

A section of the Panathenaic frieze still in its original place is discernible above the architrave supported by the inner hexastyle portico. A continuous frieze was one of the Ionic elements which Ictinus introduced into the Parthenon; he had already used it on the Temple of Apollo at Bassae (see plates 50 and 51). This frieze originally ran around the exterior of the cella wall, supported on the north and south flanks by the wall itself and on the east and west by the two hexastyle porticos. Probably carved *in situ*, in its entirety it measured five hundred twenty-three feet, seven and one-quarter inches.

In 1799 the Seventh Earl of Elgin, appointed British Ambassador to Constantinople, organized a group of specialists to take casts of sculptures and architectural details in Athens. When Lord Elgin arrived in Athens and saw the extent of the mutilation and perils to which the Parthenon marbles were daily subjected, he decided to remove, with permission from the governing Turkish authorities, whatever was feasible. Lord Elgin managed to remove two hundred forty-seven feet of the Panathenaic frieze (one hundred seventy-six feet exist elsewhere, fifty-six feet are recorded in old drawings, and around forty-five feet are totally lost), fifteen metopes from the south side, and a number of the remaining pedimental statues. One must recognize that Lord Elgin's foresightedness and generosity have preserved some of the most remarkable sculpture ever created in the Greek world.

83 A detail of the Panathenaic frieze representing horsemen from the Parthenon's west side. This section is located in its original position on the exterior of the cella wall. The subject of the frieze was the great procession that took place every four years during the Panathenaic Festival. The procession formed an honour guard for the sacred peplos, which was newly woven every four years by the *arrephoroi,* young virgins of noble parentage, and the priestess of Athena. During the Panathenaic Festival it was taken to the place of assemblage and then escorted on the masthead of a ship to the Erechtheion, where it was draped on the ancient wooden image of Athena that stood in the sanctuary of Athena Polias.

The procession on the frieze began on the southern flank and western short side, with horsemen first preparing to mount and then riding forward gathering speed and momentum. Those from the south rode towards the east façade and those from the west turned the northeast corner and rode up the northern flank toward the east façade.

The procession was interrupted and punctuated at intervals. After the horsemen, on both the north and the south friezes, came chariots with hoplites leaping on and off while they were racing. Then followed a more stately group of elders, musicians, pitcher and tray bearers, the animal victims that were to be sacrificed, the marshals of the procession, and then, turning the southeast and northeast corners, the maidens, the korai. Both groups progressed towards the middle of the frieze. Here in front of magistrates, honoured citizens, tribal heroes, and the Olympian gods, the sacred peplos was portrayed being handed to the priests, who performed the ceremonial folding. The frieze is a virtuoso example of carving, not only in its unbelievably low relief, two and one-half inches at its greatest depth, but also because Phidias managed to merge the personal and regional styles of numerous masters who must have come from all over Greece into one single, brilliant style—the Parthenon style.

As at Bassae, the frieze was placed in such a position—unlighted, half-hidden—that it could never have been properly viewed or appreciated (one can behold it better now). One must conclude, therefore, that the frieze was fashioned purely as a gift to Athena, for her personal delectation, an eternal memory frozen in marble of the procession that quadrennially took place in her honour. (*c.* 438–432 B.C.)

84 The northwest corner of the Parthenon, showing the original torsos that probably represented King Cecrops and his daughter Pandrosos, the first priestess of Athena, *in situ* on the pediment. Although the pedimental figures could be seen only from the front, every statue was perfectly finished on all sides. Since the backs of the statues were shielded from wind and rain, they are often very well preserved (one may now walk around the remaining examples, which are in the British Museum, and appreciate them from all sides, something the ancients were never able to do). Like the Panathenaic frieze, then, the sculptures should be regarded as an offering solely for the virgin goddess herself. Of course the temple itself, as well as the cult statue, were gifts to Athena, but these were to be viewed by mortal eyes and, one feels, were meant to impress mortal and deity alike.

One of the four lion-head dummy water spouts that were placed at all four corners of the temple may be seen at the corner of the north flank. Below the pediments are the relief plaques, or metopes, alternating with the triglyphs. These members, as well as others such as the regula and the guttae placed directly below the triglyphs on the architrave, are survivors of primitive wooden construction translated into stone and then, although no longer structurally necessary, retained as traditional decorative motives: the metopes were the ends of wooden beams and were covered with painted terra-cotta plaques; the triglyphs were the terminals of the alternating, thinner rafters; the guttae were originally wooden pegs.

Ninety-two sculptured metopes originally decorated the Parthenon. They were the building's earliest sculpture, because they had to be fitted into the slots between the triglyphs before the cornice was fixed in place. They are therefore probably to be dated between 447 and 438 B.C. The frieze was carved next, and then the pedimental sculptures, the latest and most developed of the Parthenon's sculptural decoration. In contrast to the low relief of the frieze, the metopes were carved in high relief, and some remain on the Parthenon, as here on the west façade. The subjects represented on the metopes were, on the east façade, the battle of the Olympian gods and the Earth-born giants; on the south, the battle between the Lapiths and the Centaurs; on the north, scenes from the Trojan legend; and on the west, the battle of the Greeks and the Amazons. Although these four subjects were frequently represented in Greek art, on the Parthenon symbolic meanings may be sought for. For example, the battle between the Lapiths and the Centaurs characterized the struggle between civilization and barbarism. The Trojan War and the battle between the Amazons and the Greeks may have had a more political meaning: both concerned Eastern peoples whose portrayal may allude to Athens' recent triumph over the Persians. The battle of the Greeks and Amazons may have had a particular and more personal meaning for Athens: Theseus had kidnapped Antiope, the sister of the Amazon queen Hippolyta; to avenge this atrocious deed the Amazons invaded Attica and, like the Persians, attacked the sacred Acropolis itself. Antiope fought and died by the side of Theseus, and Athens was single-handedly victorious over the Amazons, as she had actually been over the Persians.

85 The porch of the Erechtheion, looking towards the northwest corner of the Parthenon; between them the Panathenaic procession passed along the Sacred Way. To the east of the Parthenon, rising fifty-seven feet above the Acropolis, stood Phidias's bronze statue of Athena Promachos.

It is revealing to see two such masterpieces of Doric and Ionic architecture so juxtaposed. The use on the Erechtheion of maidens, or caryatids, as supports in place of columns had a long tradition dating back at least as far as the throne of Apollo at Amyclae, and in architecture the caryatids once thought to belong to the Cnidian Treasury and those of the Siphnian Treasury at Delphi. The south porch of the Erechtheion, however, is the supreme example; the statues may have been executed by Callimachus.

The name "Caryatid" means "maiden from Caryae," a Spartan town on the Arcadian frontier. At the annual festival of Artemis Caryatis, young girls performed a ritual dance in her honour (see the Acanthus Column at Delphi, plate 46). Certain movements and attitudes of the dance may have inspired artists to adapt the figures as architectural supports. They support an Ionic architrave that is banded with three fasciae. Usually, on an Ionic building, a continuous sculptural frieze is placed above the architrave, but since in this case it would be superfluous, the richness of the Ionic decoration was subdued.

86 View of the west façade of the Erechtheion, with the south porch of the maidens on the right and the north porch supported by six elegant, slender Ionic columns on the left. The Erechtheion is the most elaborate and unorthodox of Ionic temples. It was constructed to replace the Pisistratid Temple of Athena, whose foundations it slightly overlaps. The architect is unknown but might well have been Mnesicles, the designer of the Propylaea. Like that of the Parthenon, its official name was not originally "Erechtheion." It was the Temple of Athena Polias, and housed the sacred primitive wooden image which was quadrennially draped with the peplos carried to her with great pomp in the Panathenaic processions. It was called the Venerable Temple, in spite of its youth. The special name of its west chamber was, then, used to designate the whole building, as the name of the chamber of the virgin, Parthenon, was later applied to the whole temple.

It was constructed on two levels and had four porticos (each designed in a different style), four entrances, and a subterranean entrance under the north portico. The interior was composed of four rooms at different levels. This total irregularity of plan was due to the Athenians' desire to preserve intact certain older sacred areas, both religious and historical. Underneath the foundations lay part of the

Mycenaean palace; but, more important, it was on this site that Athena and Poseidon were said to have held their famous contest for the possession of Attica (see plate 78).

The mark of Poseidon's trident may still be seen under the north portico; his well of salt "sea" water was located under the west façade. The sacred olive tree of Athena grew where we see its present descendant, in a holy area originally sacred to Pandrosos, Athena's first priestess on the Acropolis. When the Persians burned the Acropolis, they desecrated the sacred olive tree and put it to the torch. The very next day, a green shoot appeared on its charred trunk, and during ancient times every succeeding olive tree was grafted from its predecessor. To the right of the olive tree lies the tomb of Pandrosos's father, King Cecrops, the judge of the dispute between Poseidon and Athena.

Erechtheus, the foster son of Athena (see note 66), who was cared for by the inquisitive daughters of Cecrops, was worshipped in the Erechtheion. Poseidon, Hephaestus, and Zeus also possessed shrines and altars either in the Erechtheion itself or within its sacred temenos. Holy snakes were kept in a pit under the Erechtheion, and were fed on honey cakes. One wonders whether there may not be some connection between the Minoan snake cult and the legend of the first two snake-tailed kings of Athens, Cecrops and Erechtheus, who were said to have reigned during the Mycenaean Age and were buried or worshipped in this building. To this day in some parts of Greece snakes are held in esteem and considered symbols of good fortune.

The building was erected between 421 B.C. and 405 B.C., interrupted by the Athenian expedition against Syracuse which ended in disaster for Athens. It was constructed of Pentelic marble, with the exception of the frieze, another unusual feature of this building. The frieze decorated three of the porticos, but not the porch of the maidens (see plate 85), and was executed in greyish-black Eleusinian marble; sculptured figures of white marble were separately attached to the frieze with clamps, thus giving the effect of wedgwood in marble. (421–405 B.C.)

87 "Nike," or "Victory," adjusting her sandal, from the south side of the Nike parapet. The Temple of Athena Nike was constructed on an outlying bastion (see next plate). Towards the end of the fifth century B.C. a parapet was constructed around the periphery of this bastion to protect unwary visitors from a dangerous fall. This balustrade, located on the north, west, and south sides, was subsequently decorated with one of the finest and most beautiful sculptured friezes preserved to us. It represents Nike bringing a bull to sacrifice. The Victories were depicted in various attitudes displaying the virtuoso art of carving drapery. Here the drapery falls over the figure in large cascading folds, delicately and provocatively suggesting her full, sensuous body. How far Greek sculptors had come since "The Water Carrier" (see plate 70) of only one hundred and fifty years earlier! (c. 410–400 B.C. Acropolis Museum, Athens.)

88 The Ionic Temple of Athena Nike, goddess of victory. Made of Pentelic marble, it was originally designed by the second architect of the Parthenon, Callicrates, around 449 B.C., but was not erected until the last quarter of the fifth century B.C., probably between the years 427 and 424 B.C. It was constructed over an area that had been consecrated to Athena Nike since around 550 B.C.—interestingly enough, directly on top of the Mycenaean bastions. In 448 B.C. the Mycenaean tower was covered with the present porous blocks.

The size and plan of the building were compromised by the earlier construction of the Propylaea, just as the Propylaea had been curtailed because the area had already been reserved for the erection of this temple. As it was finally executed, the temple was composed of four columns across the front (east) and the back (west)—an architectural design called "Tetrastyle Amphi-Prostyle"—and the cella consisted of a single room. It was similar in plan to the temple on the Ilissus River, now totally dismantled. The subject of the sculptured frieze which encircled the temple was scenes of combat from the battle of Plataia, which took place in 479 B.C. This was the third and last of the great battles in which Athens defeated the invading Persian army; thus this frieze claims the honour of being the first frieze known to us illustrating an actual historical event.

Sometimes the temple is referred to as the Temple of Wingless Victory (Nike Apteros) because Athena, unlike Nike (Victory), is usually not represented with wings (except sometimes in Archaic art) while Nike is always portrayed with wings.

One of the many surprises awaiting modern pilgrims to the Acropolis is the various shades of colour the Pentelic marble assumes according to the time of day and position of the sun. At sunrise the buildings are pinkish, while at noon they become almost pristine white. This photograph was taken while evening was approaching, and the marble and the porous blocks have acquired a rich honey colour.

89 The porch of the maidens and a section of the west wing of the Erectheion at sunset. The third kore from the right is a cement cast of the one that Lord Elgin carried off to the British Museum. The caryatids were copied a number of times; examples have been found in the Forum of Augustus in Rome and at Hadrian's Villa at Tivoli.

It has been suggested that these caryatids were meant to represent the arrephoroi, the weavers of Athena's peplos. The night before the great Panathenaic procession, two arrephoroi were chosen to take part in a mystic rite of ancient tradition: the priestess of Athena gave each of them mysterious objects, which were placed in a covered basket carried on their heads. They descended the Acropolis by a secret stairway, and made their way to the sanctuary of Aphrodite on the north slope. There they deposited the objects and received others to carry back to the Acropolis. Here the caryatids do carry something on their heads, but the resemblance is to capitals rather than baskets. Tempting as it may be to identify the caryatids with the arrephoroi, the latter were young girls between the ages of seven and eleven, and these maidens are in their full bloom of womanhood.

The Erechtheion did not survive untouched. In the seventh century it was turned into a Byzantine church; under Turkish domination it became a harem in 1463.

This photograph taken at twilight has captured the last rays of Helios illuminating the watchful guardians, creating a mood of mystery appropriate to the oldest and most sacred area on the Acropolis. (421–405 B.C.)

90 View of the east façade and the south flank of the Parthenon taken at sunset. After the decree of Theodosius II in A.D. 426, all pagan sanctuaries were closed. Phidias's gold and ivory cult statue of Athena Parthenos was taken to Constantinople. In A.D. 450 an apse was driven into the east end of the Parthenon (at which time the central pedimental group may have been destroyed); and the great pagan temple was converted into a Christian church. It remained so for a thousand years, until it was transformed into a mosque in 1460. At seven o'clock in the evening on September 26, 1687, a Venetian shell landed on the Parthenon, blowing up the Turkish powder magazine kept there, thus destroying much of this magnificent temple. Later, in the midst of its proud ruins, a small, insignificant mosque was constructed in the cella. Turkish houses soon clustered around the building. After the establishment of the Greek monarchy in 1832, these ugly encumbrances were removed and restoration at last began.

It is all but impossible to describe accurately the great buildings of the Acropolis. Plutarch's words, although written some 1860 years ago, remain true today: "As the works rose, shining with grandeur and possessing an inimitable grace of form, and the workmen strove to surpass one another in the beauty of their workmanship, the rapidity with which they were executed was especially marvellous. For the projects, each of which they thought would require several successive generations to reach completion, were all being completed together in the prime of one man's administration. . . . For that reason the works of Pericles are even more admired—though built in a short time, they have lasted for a long time. For, in its beauty, each work was, even at that time, ancient, and yet, in its perfection, each looks even at the present time as if it were fresh and newly built. Thus there is a certain bloom of newness in each work and an appearance of being untouched by the wear of time. It is as if some ever-flowering life and unaging spirit had been infused into the creation of these works."

73

V

DIONYSUS, POSEIDON, ASCLEPIUS, AMPHIARAUS
SOUNION, EPIDAURUS, OROPUS, THASOS

DIONYSUS

I begin to sing of ivy-crowned Dionysus, the loud-crying god, splendid son of Zeus and glorious Semele. The rich-haired Nymphs received him in their bosoms from the lord his father and fostered and nurtured him carefully in the dells of Nysa, where by the will of his father he grew up in a sweet-smelling cave, being reckoned among the immortals. But when the goddesses had brought him up, a god oft hymned, then began he to wander continually through the woody coombes, thickly wreathed with ivy and laurel. And the Nymphs followed in his train with him for their leader; and the boundless forest was filled with their outcry.

And so hail to you, Dionysus, god of abundant clusters! Grant that we may come again rejoicing to this season, and from that season onwards for many a year.
—*To Dionysus* (Homeric Hymn XXVI)

Dionysus was originally worshipped as god of wine, then vegetation, fertility, and ultimately death and the regeneration of life. He was the centre of profuse and contradictory legends; he became one of the most important of the Greek gods and was associated with various religious cults. Although his name means "the Zeus of Nysa," he was enriched by characteristics borrowed from the Cretan god Zagreus, the Phrygian god Sabazius, and the Lydian god Bassareus. According to the legend of Dionysus's birth, Hera, disguised as Beroë, Semele's nurse, persuaded Semele, the daughter of King Cadmus of Thebes and Harmonia, to demand that her supposed divine lover stand before her in all his glory to prove to her that he was truly a god. Zeus reluctantly appeared as Olympian Zeus with thunderbolt in hand, and Semele, a mortal unable to tolerate the heat of his thunderbolt, was burned to a crisp. But before she died, an ivy shoot suddenly wound around the columns of her father's palace, creating a green screen between her unborn child and Zeus's celestial fire. Zeus gathered up the unborn infant from his mother's womb and enclosed it in his own thigh. When the moment of birth arrived, Zeus, with the aid of Eilithyia, goddess of childbirth, drew Dionysus forth.

Because of this double birth, Dionysus is often called Dithyrambos, the twice-born. He became associated with death and resurrection, and those who took part in his mysteries believed that they, like him, would be reborn into an eternal life. Many festivals were held in his honour, and his worship could at times become drunken and orgiastic. Wine, symbolizing the spirit of the god, was drunk and was infused into the bodies and minds of his followers; further excited by music and dancing they would reach a state of ecstatic frenzy. In this moment of liberation animals and sometimes even hapless humans accidentally witnessing Dionysus's sacred rites might be torn to shreds. From his festivals' music, dancing, and singing developed the dithyramb—and ultimately Greek drama.

POSEIDON

I begin to sing about Poseidon, the great god, mover of the earth and fruitless sea, god of the deep who is also lord of Helicon and wide Aegae. A twofold office the gods allotted you, O Shaker of the Earth, to be a tamer of horses and a saviour of ships!

Hail, Poseidon, Holder of the Earth, dark-haired lord! O blessed one, be kindly in heart and help those who voyage in ships!

—*To Poseidon* (Homeric Hymn XXII)

Poseidon was a son of Kronos and Rhea, and an elder brother of Zeus. He was originally the god of earthquakes, and as such was Ennosigaios—the earth-shaker. He may have originally been a consort of the earth, but he soon became the god of all water.

Like all the gods, he was both benevolent and destructive. His springs fertilized the earth, but his floods destroyed. The bull was a symbol of the raging flood, and so it, like the horse, was sacred and was sacrificed to him, sometimes being thrown alive into his waters. Often vengeful and violent, Poseidon received human sacrifice as well. The dolphin and the tuna fish were among the symbols of his beneficent side as sender of favourable winds and god of the calm and peaceful waters. The pine tree, which so often grows by the seaside, was also sacred to him.

Poseidon was worshipped especially in connection with navigation, and temples were usually dedicated to him on isthmuses or promontories.

ASCLEPIUS

I begin to sing of Asclepius, son of Apollo and healer of sicknesses. In the Dotian plain fair Coronis, daughter of King Phlegyas, bare him, a great joy to men, a soother of cruel pangs.

—*To Asclepius* (Homeric Hymn XVI)

Asclepius, the god of medicine, was the son of the healing god, Apollo, and Coronis, whom he had seduced. But Coronis had been a follower of Apollo's sister, Artemis, who therefore slew her for her broken vow of chastity. When Coronis's body was placed on the funeral pyre, Apollo snatched Asclepius from her womb and gave him to the wise Centaur, Chiron, who raised him and taught him the secrets of medicinal herbs. The version told by the priests at Epidaurus, however, asserts that Coronis secretly gave birth to Asclepius on a mountain near Epidaurus—and there the child was nourished by a herd of wild goats.

Such was the skill of Asclepius as a healer that he was even able to restore the dead to life. Zeus, either from fear that Asclepius would set men forever free from death—and thus let them come too close to the immortal gods themselves—or at the instigation of Hades, god of the underworld, slew him with a thunderbolt. Apollo, in horror and revenge, killed all the Cyclops, because these giants had given Zeus the thunderbolt and had continued to forge them for him.

Asclepius was worshipped at the sources of medicinal springs, but his main sanctuaries were located on the island of Kos, Knidos, at Pergamon, and at Epidaurus, his greatest and most famous. Patients were required to sleep in a sacred building, and sometimes were given some kind of narcotic. They were informed by the priests of the sanctuary that the god would come to them in a dream, and would counsel them about their disease and the necessary cure. Perhaps it was a priest, a representative of the god, who whispered into the sleeping patient's ear. Many votive reliefs on the temples of Asclepius attest to miraculous cures—one patient was pregnant for nine years, until the god finally delivered her.

AMPHIARAUS

Amphiaraus was a great hero as well as a prophet. He took part in the Caledonian boar hunt, the voyage of the Argonauts, and the expedition of the Seven against Thebes, his last adventure. Although Amphiaraus foresaw his end he was persuaded by his wife, Eriphyle, who had been bribed by Polynices with the necklace of Harmonia (the mother of Semele), to join the war against Thebes—and thus go to certain doom. But just as the prophecy was about to come true, Zeus intervened to save the just man, hurling a thunderbolt that parted the Earth, and ordered her to swallow Amphiaraus together with his faithful charioteer. Thus Zeus made Amphiaraus immortal, and from that time on he was worshipped as an oracular god—especially at Oropus, on the frontier of Attica and Boeotia, where he had an oracular sanctuary. There dreams were interpreted and games and dramas were held in his honour.

NOTES ON THE ILLUSTRATIONS

91 A Hellenistic head of Dionysus. Dionysus was often portrayed as a mature man with a long beard, often accompanied by his drunken entourage of maenads, satyrs, nymphs, and sileni. Here, however, he is represented as young and rather effeminate, beardless, and crowned with evergreen ivy as one of the symbols of his everlasting life. This head, over life-size, portrays him with long hair tied back with two fillets; his lips are parted, and the expression on his face is rather pensive. (Late third century B.C. Parian marble. Thasos Museum.)

92 Cape Sounion, crowned by the Temple of Poseidon. When Athenians rounded this cape, the southernmost tip of Attica, they could see reflections of Apollo's rays glinting on the spear tip and gilded helmet crest of the colossal bronze statue of Athena Promachos on the Acropolis (see note and plate 85). Then they knew that they were safely home, protected under the aegis of the warrior goddess and her uncle, Poseidon.

Athena was also honoured at Sounion by a lop-sided Ionic temple that originally stood around five hundred forty yards from Poseidon's—but only a few fragments and foundation stones now remain.

93 The Doric Temple of Poseidon at Sounion. The present marble temple was probably designed by the unknown "Theseum" architect, around 444 B.C. (see plate 72). It was built over an earlier porous limestone temple erected shortly before 490 B.C. and destroyed during the Persian invasion of that year.

The plan of the temple was similar to that of the Hephaisteion: hexastyle, peripteral, with thirteen columns along the flank; it included a pronaos, a cella, and an opisthodomos. These grey-white striated columns were unusual in having only sixteen flutes instead of the usual twenty. Unlike the Hephaisteion, this temple was not embellished with interior columns, but a continuous Ionic sculptured frieze decorated the walls of the pronaos. Fragments of this frieze are preserved. The subjects represented were the adventures of Poseidon's son, Theseus, the battle of the Centaurs and Lapiths, and scenes from the struggle between the gods and the giants—a combination of subjects which decorated the Hephaisteion and the Parthenon. The metopes were not carved, but left blank.

Like Delphi (plates 34, 36, 38, 42, and 44) Bassae (plates 50 and 51), and innumerable other sites, the Temple of Poseidon at Sounion exhibits the Greeks' unquestioned genius for selecting dramatic sites of unparalleled beauty for their temples. (444–440 B.C.)

94 The foundations of the Tholos in the Sanctuary of Asclepius at Epidaurus. In the building accounts preserved to us, this tholos is referred to as the "Thymele," or altar. The foundations, fashioned of a conglomerate stone, are of the most unusual and peculiar design, composed of a series of six concentric rings. The three rings nearest the center were interrupted by doors; the other three outer rings were continuous.

The design suggests an underground labyrinth. The snake was sacred to Asclepius and when wound around a cane was his symbol. This underground maze may possibly have had something to do with a snake cult. Snakes were kept in pits in the stoa of the Asclepeum at Athens, as well as in the Erechtheion (see plate 86). Snakes, because they often live underground and emerge through the ground to cast off their skin annually and grow another one, became a symbol of the death and regeneration of life. (360–350 B.C.)

95 A restored section of the coffered ceiling of the marble Tholos in the Sanctuary of Asclepius at

Epidaurus and a Corinthian capital and column drum from its interior colonnade. According to Pausanias, the tholos was designed by Polycleitus the Younger, who had also designed the famous theatre at Epidaurus. The building, like the Tholos at Delphi (see plates 38 and 47), consisted of a circular cella with an exterior peristyle of twenty-six Doric columns. The interior was lighted by two windows, and embellished by a free-standing circle of fourteen Corinthian columns that stood on a decorative pavement of alternating black and white rhomboidal slabs. The ceiling was enhanced by coffers, out of which blossomed flowers. Pausanias also saw paintings displayed in this building and describes two by Pausias: one of an Eros, and the second of "Drunkenness" drinking from a glass.

The Corinthian capitals are among the most beautiful in existence. One of these may have been used as a model for the others. Since it was unfinished, it was subsequently buried and fortunately is perfectly preserved. (360–350 B.C. Epidaurus Museum.)

96 A section of the sima, or gutter, with a lion's-head water spout, from the Tholos at Epidaurus. The sima is decorated with a luxurious acanthus rinceau. From the calyx of the acanthus plant springs a palmette, while acanthus stalks and leaves explode and spill from the plant, spiralling and twisting across the sima. The advance of one sprig has been stopped by the lion's head, so it curls elegantly backward. On the other side of the snarling water spout a stylized flower blooms. The whole design is connected by the underlying meander border, a design most common in vase painting.

There were three other tholoi, or round buildings, located in sanctuaries—at Delphi (see plate 38), Olympia, and Samothrace. It is not yet known what purpose they served. If the subterranean labyrinth housed the sacred snakes—and since the word Thymele means altar—perhaps this type of building was used for special kinds of libations and sacrifices. (360–350 B.C. Parian marble. Epidaurus Museum.)

97 The theatre in the Sanctuary of Amphiaraus at Oropus. The theatre, nestled among pine trees, was of an unusual design. The orchestra and scene building were actually sunk below the natural surface of the ground—here the whole area of the scene building (the small area in back of the proscenium and in front of the semicircular orchestra) was excavated. Originally the scene buildings were made of wood; later, as here, of stone. At first the proscenium colonnades were usually Doric in style, but at Oropus they are in the form of semi-columns backed by rectangular piers, placed further back than the line of the columns in order to attach the painted scenery panels.

Evidence of symmetrically arranged sockets for upright timbers attests that there was also an upper wooden scene. Here gods could make their sudden "deus ex machina" appearances. (200–150 B.C.)

98 The southernmost tip of the peninsula of Sithonia, approaching the promontories of Mount Athos, and beyond, Thasos. Legend states that during the battle between the gods and giants, one of the latter, Athos by name, threw this "stone" at Poseidon.

Later, in 491 B.C., Poseidon, ever on the side of the Greeks, tried to aid them by delaying the invading Persians. While Mardonius was attempting to sail past this cape, Poseidon sent a gale that wrecked three hundred ships and killed twenty thousand men. In 480 B.C., Xerxes tried unsuccessfully to cut a canal through the peninsula to avoid having to sail around this cape and risk further trouble from Poseidon.

In Greece, the land and the sea are so closely linked one can readily understand why Poseidon and Gaea were considered to be lovers.

99 An ivory lion's head from the island of Thasos. Thasos was colonized by Ionians from the Cycladic island of Paros. Herodotus maintained that Thasos had gold mines, but her main sources of wealth were her marble, oil, and the wine sacred to Dionysus, which she exported. This commercialism brought Thasos into contact with other islands, Egypt, and the Near East. The ivory material used to carve this lion's head may well have come from a Near Eastern merchant, and its style, too, shows Near Eastern influence. This photograph reveals the open jaws, the devouring teeth, the ears laid back against the head in anger, the stylized tufted mane—and also the snarling muzzle, reflected in the glass of the showcase. (Early fifth century B.C. Thasos Museum.)

VI

DEMETER, PERSEPHONE, AND THE MYSTERY RELIGIONS
ELEUSIS, SAMOTHRACE

I begin to sing of rich-haired Demeter, awful goddess—of her and her trim-ankled daughter whom Aïdoneus rapt away, given to him by all-seeing Zeus the loud-thunderer.

Apart from Demeter, lady of the golden sword and glorious fruits, {Persephone} was playing with the deep-bosomed daughters of Oceanus and gathering flowers over a soft meadow, roses and crocuses and beautiful violets, irises also and hyacinths and the narcissus, which Earth made to grow at the will of Zeus and to please the Host of Many, to be a snare for the bloomlike girl—a marvellous, radiant flower. It was a thing of awe whether for deathless gods or mortal men to see: from its root grew a hundred blooms and it smelled most sweetly, so that all wide heaven above and the whole earth and the sea's salt swell laughed for joy. And the girl was amazed and reached out with both hands to take the lovely toy; but the wide-pathed earth yawned there in the plain of Nysa, and the lord, Host of Many, with his immortal horses sprang out upon her—the Son of Cronos, He who has many names.

He caught her up reluctant on his golden car and bare her away lamenting. . . .

To Demeter (Homeric Hymn II)

According to the Homeric Hymn, for nine days and nights Demeter roamed the earth in search of her daughter Persephone. Hecate told Demeter she had heard Persephone cry; and Helios, who had seen the incident, revealed that Hades had carried her off. Sadder still, Demeter assumed the guise of an old woman called Deo (the seeker), and wandered through city and town until she came to Eleusis. There the wife and daughters of King Celeus graciously received her, and she became a nurse for Queen Metanira's newborn son, Triptolemus (originally Demophoön). Demeter loved the child and reared him like a god, bathing him with ambrosia and at night, to burn away his mortal parts, she placed him in a fire. Metanira spied upon her, and when discovered, Demeter angrily threw down the child, relinquished her disguise, and assumed her divine stature. She said to Metanira, "Witless are you mortals and dull to foresee your lot, whether of good or evil, that comes upon you. For now in your heedlessness you have wrought folly past healing; for—be witness the oath of the gods, the relentless water of Styx—I would have made your dear son deathless and unaging all his days and would have bestowed on him everlasting honour, but now he can in no way escape death and the fates. Yet shall unfailing honour always rest upon him, because he lay upon my knees and slept in my arms. But, as the years move round and when he is in his prime, the sons of the Eleusinians shall ever wage war and dread strife with one another continually. Lo! I am that Demeter who has share of honour and is the greatest help and cause of joy to the undying gods and mortal men. But now, let all the people build me a great temple and an altar below it and beneath the city and its sheer wall upon a rising hillock above Callichorus. And I myself will teach my rites, that hereafter you may reverently perform them and so win the favour of my heart."

The temple was built, but Demeter still grieved and would not permit the ground to bear grain or fruit. "So she would have destroyed the whole race of man with cruel famine and have robbed them who dwell on Olympus of their glorious right of gifts and sacrifices, had not Zeus perceived and marked this in his heart."

Zeus sent Iris to summon Demeter to Olympus, but she refused to come. Then all the gods brought gifts, but no one could persuade Demeter to change her mind. So Zeus sent Hermes down to the Land of Shades, to persuade Hades to give up his bride Persephone.

Hermes spoke to Hades: "Dark-haired Hades, ruler over the departed, father Zeus bids me bring noble Persephone forth from Erebus unto the gods, that her mother may see her with her eyes and cease from her dread anger with the immortals; for now she plans an awful deed, to destroy the weak tribes of earth-born men by keeping seed hidden beneath the earth, and so she makes an end of the honours of the undying gods. For she keeps fearful anger and does not consort with the gods, but sits aloof in her fragrant temple, dwelling in the rocky hold of Eleusis."

Hades agreed, but first gave Persephone a pomegranate to eat. Then with Hermes he returned Persephone to her sorrowing mother at the mouth of the cave called the Ploutonion, near Demeter's Temple at Eleusis. Since Persephone had tasted of the pomegranate seed Zeus decreed to Demeter "that her daughter should go down for the third part of the circling year to darkness and gloom, but for the two parts should live with her mother and the other deathless gods. . . ."

Then Demeter "made fruit to spring up from the rich lands, so that the whole wide earth was laden with leaves and flowers. Then she went, and to the kings who deal justice, Triptolemus and Diocles, the horse driver, and to doughty Eumolpus, and Celeus, leader of the people, she showed the conduct of her rites and taught them all her mysteries, to Triptolemus and Polyxeinus and Diocles also—awful mysteries which no one may in any way transgress or pry into or utter, for deep awe of the gods checks the voice. Happy is he among men upon earth who has seen these mysteries; but he who is uninitiate and who has no part in them, never has lot of like good things once he is dead, down in the darkness and the gloom."

The author of this hymn and the time of its composition are unknown, but scholars have begun to seriously consider it the official story of the Eleusinian tradition, perhaps first preserved in written form during the end of the seventh century B.C.

Demeter was the daughter of Kronos and Rhea, and sister to Zeus. Her name may have meant "mother-earth," signifying that she was goddess of agriculture. Zeus desired Demeter, but she resisted him. He, however, took her by turning himself into a bull, and she became the mother of Kore, or Persephone. The legend retold above in the Homeric Hymn symbolized the eternal rotation of the seasons. For when Persephone descended into Hades, Demeter sorrowed and the land became bare and fruitless—winter; but when Persephone returned four months later, Demeter, full of joy, caused the seed to grow and the earth to be covered with flowers—spring.

As goddess of agriculture, Demeter also came to be associated with law, order, and marriage. As the goddess of fertility, Demeter was associated with Poseidon, and in many regions, such as Arcadia, Poseidon as the god of fertilizing water was actually regarded as the father of Persephone. This is probably a vestige of an older religion, when Poseidon was considered to be the consort of Earth. Demeter, as goddess of the earth—to whom the seed is consigned but also to whom the dead are committed—was connected with the lower world, and worshipped as Chthonia.

In later times, she was often confused with Gaea, Rhea, and Cybele. Fruit, grain, and honeycombs, as well as the cow and the sow (as symbols of productivity) were among the offerings made to her. Demeter was often represented with ears of corn, symbol of fertility and fruitfulness. Other emblems had a more mystic meaning: the torch was used in her mysteries, and the serpent symbolized a renewal of life.

Although Eleusis was inhabited since Early Helladic times, by popular tradition the cult of Demeter seems to have been introduced during the fifteenth century B.C. There are numerous references in the Homeric Hymn that could well describe a Mycenaean house and the Mycenaean political system. But where did the cult originate? Cretan, Egyptian, or Minoan origins have been proved unlikely.

Recent excavations have shown that the oldest temple of Demeter, which dates from Mycenaean times, was in the form of a Greek-type megaron, and the name "Demeter" is purely Greek. A north Greek origin, perhaps Thessaly or Thrace, has been suggested. Eumolpus—mentioned in the Homeric Hymn and apparently the first celebrant of the mysteries at Eleusis—and his mother Chione were said to have come from Thrace. And, according to tradition, the Thracians came to the help of the Eleusinians during the war with Athens. Although the origin of the cult remains as unknown as the details of the rituals themselves, for almost two thousand years before it was replaced by Christianity the Eleusinian Mysteries provided the Greeks with some sort of belief in rebirth and eternal life beyond the grave.

The Eleusinian tradition stated that Demeter herself introduced her cult at Eleusis. Unlike other pagan religious rites, it was not open to the general public but only to those who had been initiated by officially having performed certain rituals prescribed by tradition. Furthermore, the initiate was sworn not to divulge the secrets. "No one in any way may transgress or pry into or utter."

At first the cult was local, but during the eighth century, the Geometric period, it began to expand. Perhaps the Proerosia, a festival and sacrifice, may have been established around 760 B.C. During that period, Greece suffered a severe famine. The Delphic Oracle ordered the Athenians to offer a sacrifice to Demeter in the name of all the Greeks before the beginning of the ploughing season, and the famine miraculously came to an end. From that time on, the Greek states sent annual offerings of the first fruits of the year to Eleusis as a token of gratitude.

The cult eventually became Panhellenic. By the time the Romans had adopted it, Eleusis had become one of the most important religious centres of the pagan world. The secrecy of all details pertaining to the cult of Demeter was severely enforced by the state (the mysteries of the Orphic religion are better known and should not be confused with those of Eleusis). Alcibiades was accused of violating this oath of secrecy, and popular though he was, his property was confiscated and all priests and priestesses were instructed to pronounce curses against him.

The mysteries were celebrated in two parts. The first was held in public and included the taking of the *Hiera,* or holy objects of Demeter, from the Anaktoron (the house of the lords) at Eleusis to Athens; the sacred proclamation (see below); the descent to the sea; the sacrifice of piacular pigs; the *pompe* (procession) that carried the statue of Iacchos from Athens to Eleusis; and the appearance of the Hierophant (the high priest), the Dadouchos (the torchbearer, second in rank to the Hierophant), and other priests in their vestments. There are references to details of the second part in ancient literary sources—Plutarch's mention of the brilliant light in the midst of which the Hierophant appeared when the Anaktoron was opened; allusions to the great alternation of moods and feelings experienced by initiates; a statement attributed to Aristotle that they suffered rather than learned—but none mention the rituals involved.

Since the myth of Triptolemus receiving the grain from Demeter appeared so often in art, it may safely be presumed that it formed no part of the mysteries. It would be impossible to describe all the priests, officials, and known services in detail, so only the most important facts are given here.

The Hierophant came from the family of the Eumolpids and held office for life. In fact, most of the priestly offices for women and men alike were filled by members of the Eumolpids and the Ceryces families.

The chief divinities were Demeter; her daughter, Kore, or Persephone; Pluton, the god of the Underworld; Iacchos, a divine personification of the shouting and enthusiasm that characterized the procession from Athens to Eleusis.

The mysteries included degrees of initiation: *katharmos,* initial purification; *teletis paradosis,* mystic communion or communication; *epopteia,* or revelation and the sight of holy objects; and *Anadesis,* the crowning with garlands, which afterwards became the badge of the initiate. The first three were apparently the main degrees. The first, the preliminary initiation into the Lesser Mysteries, was celebrated once a year in early spring (but if the crowds were large, it was celebrated twice). We know very little of what transpired, but it appears to have been a ritual that aimed at complete purification of the candidate. The second degree was the initiation into the Greater Mysteries, the *telete;* the third degree, the *epopteia,* was the highest. The Greater Mysteries were celebrated once a year, and every fourth year with great splendour during the end of September and the beginning of October. Pilgrims came to these annual festivals from all over the world.

The mysteries took nine days, possibly symbolizing the amount of time it took Demeter to learn where Persephone had been abducted. The first day began with a sacred proclamation. Everyone who had "clean hands" and "intelligible speech" (meaning Greek; i.e., no "barbarians"), who was "pure from all pollution and whose soul is conscious of no evil, and who has lived well and justly" could proceed with the initiation; the rest had to abstain. Anyone not absolved from the guilt of homicide was excluded from participation.

The second day Athens echoed with shouts: "To the sea, O Mystai (initiates)!" Then the initiates bathed in the sea, considered to be immaculate and to have cleansing powers that could purify man from evil. They also took with them a pig and bathed it, purifying it, and then sacrificed it, for the pig's blood was considered to have the power to absorb the impure spirit inhabiting human beings.

The third day may have been spent sacrificing on behalf of the city. The rites were repeated on the fourth day, called the *Epidauria,* or the *Asclepia,* in honour of Asclepius. According to legend, he had arrived late for the proclamation and purification in the sea. In commemoration of this, then, the rites were repeated for latecomers; those who had already taken part in them remained at home.

The fifth day was the culmination of the rites and festivities in Athens—the day of the procession to Eleusis and the return of the *Hiera* to Eleusis.

The sixth day, the first day at Eleusis, was probably passed in partial or total fasting, in imitation of the goddess Demeter, who had also fasted during her search for Persephone—and like her they may have drunk the *cyceon,* a special potion of meal mixed with water and soft mint. The ceremonies performed on the sixth night may have consisted of three things. The first was a *dromena,* or a sacred presentation of the story of Demeter and Persephone. This pageant was accompanied by music and singing, but no dialogue. Perhaps this took place in the Telesterion, or both inside the Telesterion and outside in various parts of the sanctuary, so that the *mystai* could follow the goddess in her wanderings (as Christians follow the Via Cruxis during the Passion of Christ) to enable them to participate more fully in the goddess's sorrows. Then they may all have assembled at the mouth of the Ploutonion Cave (see plate 102) to see and to welcome Persephone on her return from the lower world.

It has been suggested that a *hieros gamos*—a sacred marriage—took place between the Hierophant and the priestess. At one point during the services, initiates looked up to the sky and cried, "Rain"; then down to the earth crying "Conceive"; and conceivably the *mystai* shouted these words while the Hierophant and priestess were enacting this rite of fertilization in an underground chamber. But excavations have proved that there was no underground chamber. Furthermore, if these were the most sacred words of the holy ceremony, one wonders why they were carved on a common well-head near the Dipylon Gate in Athens in full view of everyone—when the slightest breaking of the oath of secrecy was punished so severely.

It has also been suggested that a sacramental banquet took place. If there was such a meal, it probably consisted of the *cyceon,* and probably preceded the ceremonies. It is not known what words or phrases were spoken during the *legomena* (words that were uttered during the ceremonies of initiation) or the *deiknymena* (the revelation of the sacred objects) or what objects were shown. Perhaps the sacred ritual objects were Mycenaean relics handed down since the beginning of Demeter's cult. Such objects would be foreign and "awe-inspiring" to the Greeks of later eras.

The *epopteia,* or highest degree of initiation, was not a necessary sequel to the *telete,* but those who wished to take it had to wait until one year after their original initiation in the *telete.* Once again, what transpired is purely conjectural, but apparently other sacred objects, *Hiera,* were exhibited and initiates gained a fuller understanding of the meaning of these ancient holy rites.

There seems to be no Dionysian influence detectable in the Eleusinian ritual. The last, or eighth, day of the initiation at Eleusis was apparently devoted mainly to the dead, who were remembered with certain rites and libations. On the ninth day, the *mystai* returned home.

Like all pagan sanctuaries, Eleusis suffered with the coming of Christianity. The Eleusinian mysteries enjoyed a revival under Julian the Apostate, but Theodosius snuffed them out with his edict closing all pagan sanctuaries. The early Christians in the fifth century A.D. finished the destruction begun by the hordes of Alaric in A.D. 395. They built their church near the ruined temples of the mysteries, and buried their dead in the holy area, thus polluting this earth sacred to Demeter.

The goddess Demeter has indeed kept her mysteries secret, and what they were we cannot yet know, but Sophocles wrote, "Thrice happy are those mortals, who, having seen those rites, depart for Hades; for to them alone is it granted to have true life there; to the rest all there is evil."

The Sanctuary on the island of Samothrace, like Eleusis, was famous in antiquity for its cult of the Great Gods *(Megaloi Theoi).* This cult included certain "mysteries" into which any person, king or slave, might be initiated. The Sanctuary of the Great Gods did not, like Eleusis, belong officially to a Greek city-state; but like Olympia and Delphi it was international in character and enjoyed a universal prestige. A number of deities were associated with a Great Mother who was related to the Earth Mother of Anatolia, the Phrygian Cybele, and the Trojan Mother of Mount Ida. Her origin was pre-Greek. In the Samothracians' native language she was called "Axeiros," but the Greek settlers who arrived on Samothrace around 700 B.C. associated her with their Earth Mother, Demeter.

Two other nature deities were worshipped on Samothrace. They originally may have represented another facet of the Earth Mother: Hecate, a great nature deity invoked by the name of Cerynthia, and Aphrodite Cerynthia. An ithyphallic fertility god called Kadmilos, whom the Greeks identified with Hermes, may have been Axeiros's consort. Two more ithyphallic youths, the Cabiri, equated with Greek heavenly twins, the Dioscuri, were also worshipped. These Cabiri may originally have been the founders of Samothrace, the heroic brothers Aëtion and Dardanus (after whom the Dardanelles are named). Two more deities, the rulers of the underworld known at Samothrace as Axiokersos and Axiokersa (whom the Greeks identified with Hades and Persephone) completed the circle of the Great Gods.

The public rites that were practised in the sanctuary at Samothrace were probably similar to those of any other Greek sanctuary, including the sacrifice of sheep and pigs (for the underworld deities), libations, and prayers. Ordinary pilgrims and, at least from the third century B.C., ambassadors *(theoroi)* came from all over the known world to celebrate the great annual festival. It is possible that this festival may have survived in the feast of Hagia Paraskevi, which takes place July 26 and to which people still come from various towns in Thrace and from towns and villages on the island of Samothrace itself to worship, celebrate, and dance underneath plane trees near the old port of the ancient city.

During the celebration, the legend of Hades' rape of Persephone was performed in a sacred drama. The mysteries of the Great Gods became famous and were venerated as early as the fifth century B.C. throughout the Greek world. They were catholic in that all who wished to be initiated could be. At Eleusis, by contrast, only Greek-speaking people were permitted initiation. Furthermore, the Eleusinian initiation took place once a year at a prescribed time. On Samothrace anybody seeking to be initiated could be so on any day of the year. There were two stages or degrees of initiation, the first the *myesis,* and the second the *epopteia.* At Eleusis obtaining both degrees had to be separated by a year's interval; on Samothrace both could be obtained on the same day.

As at Eleusis, the mysteries took place at night by the light of torches. At some point, every *mystes* carried a lamp and consumed a sacrificial meal. This meal may not have formed an actual part of the mysteries themselves; it could have preceded or followed the initiation. An inscription describes the priest speaking to the *mystai,* saying, "Take, eat, take, drink." Many drinking vessels (*skyphoi* and *kantharoi*) and dishes have been excavated with inscriptions designating them as the property of the gods.

The initiates also apparently wore wreaths. Preparation for the initiation rites may have taken place in a small building called the *Hiera Oikia* (Sacred House). Apparently the *mystes* received his lamp, was dressed in white garments with a purple scarf tied about his waist, and was taken into a rectangular building called the Anaktoron, where he performed certain libations. Then, seemingly, he was taken into a sacred back room, or inner sanctum of the building, a room that no one but the initiated could enter, and there he was shown certain objects. What their nature was is unknown—but Varro, a distinguished Roman scholar of the first century B.C., states that he saw sacred symbols that he interpreted as representing Heaven and Earth.

The *mystes* may then have returned to the sacred house, where he received a certificate of initiation. After this he could proceed to the higher degree of the epopteia, which was celebrated in a temple-like structure called the Hieron (see plates 104 and 107.)

None but the initiated could enter this sacred building, and even a *mystes* seems to have had to undergo some sort of public questioning by the priest, and to have had to confess publicly in order to try to receive absolution. Once he entered the building he again performed purification and lustration rites, and then a sacrifice, perhaps of birds over the sacred hearth, or *eschara,* in the centre of the cella. Then the *epoptes* may have been seated to witness the revelation of symbols. In the third century A.D. alterations were made to the temple to include the *taurobolia* or *criobolia* of the Anatolian Earth Mother, Magna Mater. During the ceremony the initiate descended into a pit or crypt at the southern apse end of the Hieron, and the blood of the sacrificial victim was poured over his head in a baptismal rite.

As at Eleusis, the initiates were sworn to secrecy. While at Eleusis the initiate was promised a happy life, no such evidence has yet been found on Samothrace, though it would seem a logical parallel. On Samothrace, initiates received a purple scarf that would protect them from the perils on the sea; and the magnetic iron rings fashioned out of Samothracian magnetite were probably another symbol of protective power.

NOTES ON THE ILLUSTRATIONS

100 A detail of the grand relief of Eleusis, representing Demeter, Triptolemus, and Persephone. In the Homeric Hymn, Demeter showed the Eleusinian Triptolemus "the conduct of her rites and taught . . . all her mysteries." According to the Athenian version, Triptolemus was the son of King Celeus and Queen Metanira of Eleusis. By the sixth century B.C. the Athenians believed that Demeter had sent him travelling throughout the world to teach man the secrets of agriculture, such as how to cultivate grain. Demeter gave him a chariot drawn by winged dragons (sometimes this scene is portrayed on black-figured and red-figured vases) and wheat, with which, wafted through the sky, he sowed the whole inhabited earth.

The subject of this marble relief deals with Triptolemus's great mission. The hero stands between Demeter and her daughter, Persephone. He is represented as a young boy, possibly either to symbolize

the long journey that lies ahead of him, or because mortals are children in the eyes of the gods.

He wears sandals (not shown) and a traveller's cloak over his right shoulder to indicate his future journey. A matronly, dignified Demeter with hair flowing holds the sceptre in her left hand, and the life-nourishing seeds that will bring health and well-being to mankind in her right hand. Persephone stands behind Triptolemus, holding her torch in her left hand, and is represented in the act of crowning Triptolemus with a wreath, which was originally painted.

An exact Roman copy of this relief is on exhibition in the Metropolitan Museum of Art in New York City. (*c.* 450–440 B.C. National Museum, Athens.)

101 Proto-Attic amphora by the "Polyphemus Painter," found at Eleusis. While Corinth was developing the so-called "Orientalizing" style, Athens was evolving another style, the "proto-Attic," characterized by a new grandeur and monumentality of design. This amphora also served as the tomb of a young boy about ten to twelve years old. It stands approximately four feet eight inches high. The entire surface is decorated with figural or floral designs, painted in black with highlights or touches of white. The story of Perseus, aided by Athena, slaying Medusa and pursued by Medusa's sisters, the Gorgons, is painted on the body (not shown). A ferocious lion whose body is painted in solid black silhouette (the head is reserved, or unglazed, in order to accentuate such details as the eye, the muzzle, and the teeth) is depicted attacking a wild boar on the shoulder of the amphora.

On the neck of the amphora, Odysseus and his companions are represented blinding the one-eyed giant (Cyclops) Polyphemus, a son of Poseidon, who had managed to imprison Odysseus and his companions in his cave along with his own sheep. A man-eater, Polyphemus had consumed several of Odysseus's entourage. The wily hero managed to make Polyphemus drunk with wine, and while he was thus in a stupor Odysseus blinded him. In agony Polyphemus stationed himself at the mouth of his cave in order not to let any man escape—but when the morning came, and it was the hour to let his flocks go to pasture, Polyphemus released them, not knowing that the cunning Odysseus and his men were clinging to the sheep, underneath their bellies. Thus Odysseus and his friends were saved. Here the hero is painted in outline filled in with white to distinguish him from his companions, and to add interest to the design. He is shown next to the seated giant, who holds a *skyphos* (wine cup) in his right hand.

The background is reserved and filled with ornamental designs, whose origins may have been derived from imported Near Eastern textile embroideries. This amphora is one of the finest examples of the proto-Attic style. (675–650 B.C. Eleusis Museum.)

102 In the foreground, the Lesser Propylaea; in the background the Ploutonion or cave, entrance to the Underworld at Eleusis. This propylaea formed the entrance to the Eleusinian sanctuary itself, and un-initiates were forbidden entry on pain of death. Through it passed the *mystai,* or initiates. Perhaps at the outer gate they were checked and screened, perhaps their wreathes of myrtle were here replaced with ribbons, symbol of their consecration to the deities. The paving slabs of the Sacred Way in the foreground date from the Roman period. Because secrecy was demanded in all things pertaining to the sacred rites of Demeter on pain of her displeasure and punishment by the state, Pausanias does not describe or discuss any of the buildings within the sanctuary of Demeter at Eleusis.

During the sacred drama, or *dromena,* it is possible that the initiates wandered throughout the sanctuary, helping Demeter to search for her lost daughter, and eventually waited at the mouth of the Ploutonion for Persephone's return. Here they could await her arrival and observe her actually emerging from the Underworld. After this supreme dramatic moment, they may have accompanied her amidst rejoicing and lighted torches to the Telesterion (or hall of mysteries or initiation), where she was reunited with her mother. Such a pageant enacted at night, alternating between darkness, sorrow, searching and brilliant light, happiness, and fulfillment, must have evoked strong emotional reactions. As Pindar wrote, "Happy is he who, having seen these rites, goes below the hollow earth; for he knows the end of life and he knows its god-sent beginning."

103 The west section of the Telesterion at Eleusis, seen from south to north. Scholars have postulated that during the enactment of the *dromena,* sacred drama of Demeter and Persephone, initiates descended into Hades along a tortuous path, and were shown scenes and felt and heard terrors symbolic of death and visited the king and queen of the Underworld; they then were reborn. But romantic and dramatic as this may sound, no underground chambers have been found in the Telesterion.

Also, there are no traces of cuttings for machinery and apparatus with which to produce apparitions. In fact, one gathers from the Homeric Hymn that the mysteries were not meant to frighten but to instruct. The Telesterion actually dates back to the Mycenaean period, though not in its present form. There is also evidence of a Geometric building; an Archaic building; one constructed by Pisistratus and destroyed by Xerxes; another structure begun by Themistocles or Cimon to replace the Pisistratid building; and, finally, the great building of the Periclean period designed by Ictinus with the help of other architects (Coroebos, Metagenes, and Xenocles), which is four times the size of the Archaic building.

This great building was approximately one hundred seventy square feet internally, with seven rows of six columns. The remains of several of these columns are visible in this photograph. The lighting of the interior may have been effected by the use of clerestory windows. (The Telesterion-type building is not peculiar to Eleusis; there was one at Phyle and probably one also at Thoricos.) The building was preceded, at least in later times, by a prostyle porch consisting of twelve columns (dodecastyle). The back of the building—the western section—was cut out of the virgin rock; there were two doors to the building on each of the three free sides. There were eight rows of steps on all four sides. In some spots these steps were cut from the living rock (as here on the west side); others were constructed. These were no doubt used by the initiates in order to witness the ceremony; three thousand people could congregate at one time in the building. The building was also restored during the Roman period.

Lying under the various foundations of the later Telesteria is a Mycenaean megaron of the fifteenth century B.C. It is tempting to connect this building with the very temple that Demeter requested to have built, recorded in the Homeric Hymn.

104 A view of the Sanctuary of Samothrace, with Mount Phengari (the mountain of the moon) in the background, and the restored columns of the north or main façade of the Hieron with the foundations of the round building, or tholos, called the Arsinoeion (289–281 B.C.) in the foreground. Homer describes Poseidon seated on top of a mountain on Samothrace watching the Trojan War: "But the lord, the shaker of the earth, kept no careless watch. Marveling at the warfare and the battle, he sat high on the topmost peak of wooded Thracian Samos, for thence all Ida was plainly seen, and plainly seen were the city of Priam and the ships of the Achaeans. Forth from the sea he came, and there he sat, and he pitied the Achaeans, who were being overpowered by the Trojans, and he was sternly indignant at Zeus. Then down from the rugged mountain he went with swift strides."

Legend states that the Sanctuary at Samothrace was originally founded by Amazons under the leadership of Queen Myrina. The Amazons had already swept through Asia Minor and conquered several of the Aegean islands. They had just subdued the island of Lesbos and were sailing away when Myrina was caught in a storm; after she had offered prayers for her safety to the Mother of the Gods, she was carried to one of the uninhabited islands. In obedience to a vision that came to her in a dream, she made the island sacred to this goddess, and set up altars there, offering magnificent sacrifices. She also gave it the name of Samothrace, which means "sacred island" in Greek, although some historians say that it was formerly called Samos and was then given the name of Samothrace by the Thracians who at one time dwelt on it. However, after the Amazons had returned to the continent, the myth, in the words of Diodorus, relates, ". . . the Mother of the gods, well pleased with the island, settled on it certain other people, and also her own sons, who are known by the name of Corybantes—who their father was is handed down in their initiation as a matter not to be divulged; and she taught the mysteries which are now celebrated on the island, and ordained by law that the sacred area should enjoy the right of sanctuary."

The Hieron as it stands now was built during the last quarter of the fourth century B.C.; a fifth-century and an earlier Archaic building preceded it on the same site. The building was rectangular, long and narrow. There was no peristyle, but its main north façade was decorated by a six-columned porch in Doric style. The rear of the building terminated in an apse that was masked on the exterior, giving the impression of a simple rectangular structure. In this building was celebrated the highest degree of the mysteries, the *epopteia*.

105 A view of the Samothracian landscape near the harbor of Cameriotissa. The early history of Samothrace is still unexplored. Sporadic finds indicate that the island was probably inhabited from the Neolithic Age. Greek colonists seem to have arrived around 700 B.C., and a town near the sanctuary sprang up. It became strong, prosperous, and powerful, a city-state in its own right, and dominated part of the Thracian coast near Maroneia and Ainos. Thus Samothrace controlled the sea lanes leading to the Dardanelles, but she was eclipsed by Athens in the fifth century and became a minor city. After this it was the fame of her mystery religions that attracted visitors to the island. Prince Philip of Macedon, while being initiated into the mysteries, fell in love with a princess, Olympias, from faraway Epirus, and married her; the son she bore him was Alexander the Great.

Samothrace was strategically placed and became a naval base for many of the Hellenistic rulers. Because of her sacrosanct character, she was also a refuge for political exiles. Many illustrious visitors came to Samothrace, including Saint Paul. In her later history she suffered variously from pirates and earthquakes. A small community continued to live on the island during the Byzantine period. She eventually fell under the suzerainty of the Genoese lords, the Gattelusi. No historical records exist for the years from A.D. 1500 to 1800, but with the dramatic discovery of the Winged Victory of Samothrace in 1863, she once more regained her earlier prominence.

The waters appear to be serene and calm, and the wind is still. But this appearance is deceptive, for when Poseidon stirs the water and Boreas blows, no creature, man or beast, is able to approach this sacred island.

106 Part of the frieze of dancing girls from the Temenos on Samothrace. Professor Karl Lehmann has suggested that a ritual drama representing a sacred marriage (*hieros gamos*) was performed in this precinct, which was built over an old and sacred sacrificial area. He believes that the "search for the vanished maiden which was undoubtedly followed by a celebration with the underworld god, represented the legendary wedding of Kadmos and Harmonia," which the Samothracians maintain took place on Samothrace, and the Thebans at Thebes.

Diodorus wrote, "This wedding of Cadmus and

Harmonia was the first, we are told, for which the gods provided the marriage feast, and Demeter (enamored of Iasion) presented the fruit of the grain, Hermes a lyre, Athena the renowned necklace and a robe and flutes, and Electra the sacred rites of the great Mother of the Gods, as she is called, together with cymbals and kettledrums and the ecstatic revelers of her ritual; and Apollo played on the cithara and the Muses on their flutes, and the rest of the gods spoke them fair and gave the pair their aid in the celebration of the wedding. . . ."

Possibly this frieze of dancing maidens alludes to the sacred wedding. A sacred dance is still performed today during a Greek Orthodox wedding. The priest himself leads the bride and groom in a dance; they circle the altar three times, while rose petals are thrown on them by the members of the family and friends.

Although this marble frieze probably dates between 340 and 330 B.C., the very mannered pose of the dancers and their drapery are examples of the fourth century Archaistic style. Perhaps this was deliberate, alluding to the ancient traditions connected with the holy wedding and the wedding dance. (Samothrace Museum.)

107 A view of the restored capital and top drums of the main façade of the Hieron, and the slopes of Hagios Giorgios behind. This photograph recalls Professor Lehmann's description of the great Earth Mother, "an all-powerful ruler of a wild mountainous world; she was worshipped at sacred rocks, near which or upon which sacrifices were brought to her. . . . A curious feature of the cult of the mother of the rocks here is that she manifested her power, which was immanent in stones, in lodestones of magnetic iron of which rings were fashioned. Worn by the worshippers, they tied them to the Great Goddess."

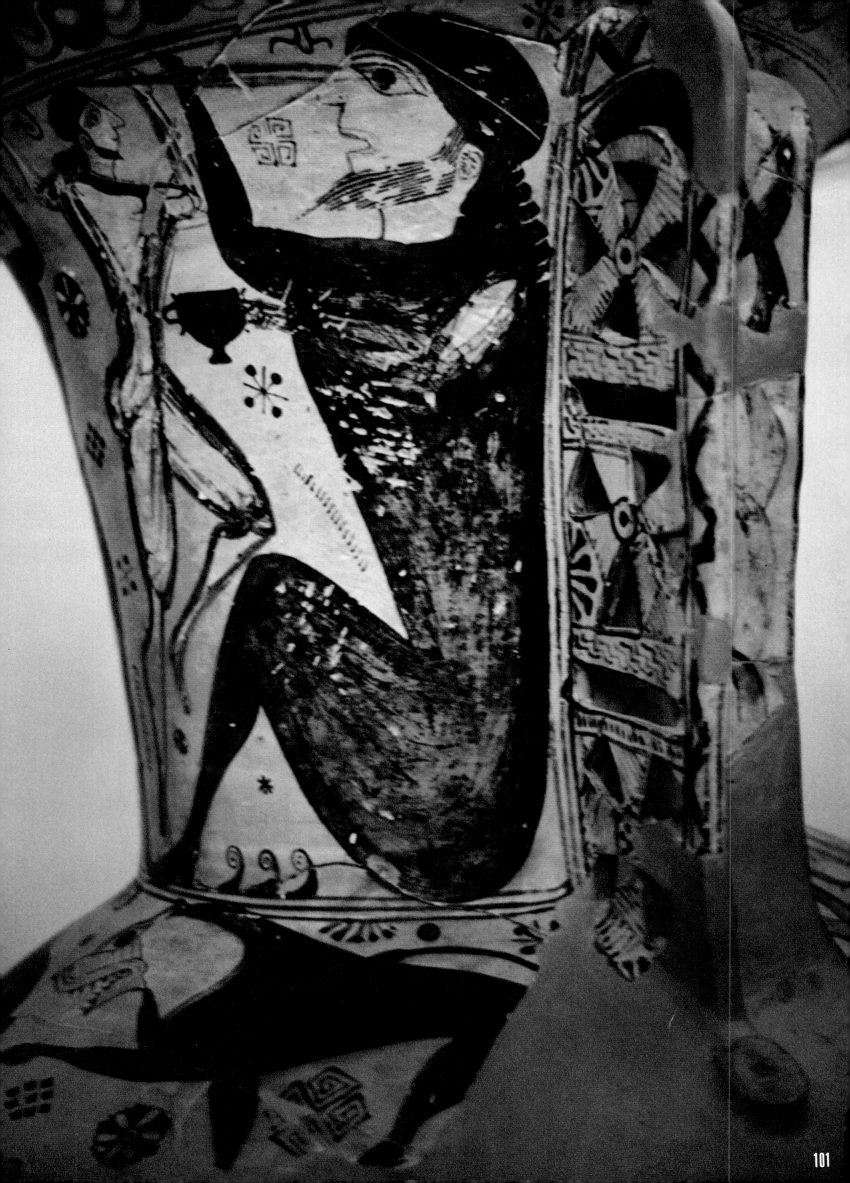

VII

CHRISTIANITY
HOSIOS LOUKAS, DAPHNI, MISTRA, MOUNT ATHOS, MYKONOS, SIPHNOS, THERA, SERIPHOS

I believe in one God the Father Almighty, Maker of heaven and earth, And of all things visible and invisible:

And in one Lord Jesus Christ, the only-begotten Son of God; Begotten of his Father before all worlds, God of God, Light of Light, Very God of very God; Begotten, not made; Being of one substance with the Father; By whom all things were made: Who for us men and for our salvation came down from heaven, And was incarnate by the Holy Ghost of the Virgin Mary, And was made man....

Nicene Creed

From Palestine, Christianity gradually spread throughout the Mediterranean world, growing increasingly more influential. Constantine the Great, who made Byzantium the capital of the Roman Empire, though still promoting the imperial cult, had Christianity officially recognized and was himself converted on his deathbed. Worship in temples and sanctuaries was permitted to continue until the decree of Theodosius I in A.D. 381 prohibiting the public celebration of pagan rites. The final blow to paganism was delivered by Theodosius II in A.D. 426, when he ordered the closing of all pagan sanctuaries. Some of the ancient temples, such as the Parthenon and the Hephaisteion, were transformed into Christian churches or used as quarries to supply material for later construction. Sometimes Christian churches were erected over ancient sites of worship, as at Daphni, preserving their sacred traditions.

Christ said, "I have not come to change but to render more perfect." Indeed, Christianity slowly emerged not as an entirely new religion but as one based heavily on its predecessors, particularly Judaism; as the Church gained more converts many pagan influences also permeated the ritual. It is almost impossible to assess the extent to which the symbolic Christian ceremony was adapted from the Eleusinian, Orphic, Dionysiac, and Eastern practices—but what follower of Dionysus, what Eleusinian or Samothracian initiate would not have understood the symbolism of the Holy Eucharist, the wine and bread, or Christ's words, "I am the resurrection and the life, he that believeth in me though he die yet shall he live again"? Many Christian saints assumed the characteristics and duties of various pagan gods and in many areas of the world, particularly Greece and Italy, local rites that had originated in pagan practice continue to be celebrated.

In Greece to this day, the snake is believed to bring good luck, especially a hearth snake living under one's house. Lambs, goats, roosters are still sacrificed and dragged bleeding around the foundations of a new building, while the priest benignly blesses the proceedings, intermittently flicking drops of holy water from a bunch of basil leaves. And during the wedding ceremony, the ancient dance of Hymen, the God of Marriage, is celebrated by the priest, bride, and bridegroom.

In pagan times the vine and its liquor were believed to be the gifts of the resurrected god, Dionysus— the spirit of the god was infused into man through the drinking of his wine—while today in the Greek Orthodox and Roman Catholic rituals during the celebration of the Holy Eucharist the wine and bread are miraculously turned into the body and blood of the sacrificed Christ. (The Roman Catholic Church serves only the host, the bread, arguing that the blood is inherent in the body; the Greek Orthodox Church serves only the wine. The bread may optionally be taken upon leaving the church.)

Perhaps the most primitive aspect of present-day Greek religion is that during menstruation a Greek

Orthodox woman is not permitted to eat from the Lord's table or to kiss the icons or touch any of the sacred objects in the church. Again recalling ancient Greek ritual, in Greek Orthodox practice on Good Friday an effigy of Christ is crucified and then removed from the cross, carried around the church, and laid into his tomb.

In yet another Greek practice reminiscent of pagan rites, forty days after the death of a person his family and friends eat cakes called *kolyva,* made of wheat grains and pomegranate seeds. Surely this not only descends from the ancient Greek funeral banquet and custom of eating for the dead, but is also a direct allusion to the idea of rebirth and regeneration of life, a reminder that the goddess of the Underworld, Persephone, consumed pomegranate seeds during her sojourn in the realm of Hades. It was, of course, because of this that she was forced to remain in the Underworld for four months of the year, thus causing winter upon earth. The pomegranate became one of Persephone's attributes; its many seeds signified the fertility and rebirth of life that nature enjoyed at Persephone's return in the spring (a ceramic vessel in the form of a pomegranate was often given as a wedding present in ancient Greece). It also alluded to the doleful time she must spend in the world of shades, when the earth was dead.

Throughout the Christian world the Virgin Mary presides over many facets of life, but in Greece she is also venerated as a protectress in time of war, just as Athena was by the ancient Greeks. Reminiscent of Athena, who was wont to appear to warriors to inspire and urge them on to victory, so during World War II Greek soldiers fighting in Albania reported seeing a vision of the Virgin, who encouraged them to resist the enemy.

Christian representational art followed the pattern set by its pagan Roman predecessor. Christ and His heavenly retinue were glorified in painting and sculpture in the same visual idiom that during paganism had been reserved for the emperor and his court. The stories of the Gospel were whenever possible retold in terms of imperial ceremonial art. In the beginning, this art was mainly narrative and didactic, i.e., its purpose was to present in visual form what the illiterate were unable to read in books. But from the sixth century onwards, icons (i.e., images) of Christ, the Virgin, and the saints increasingly became objects of worship, just as statues of the pagan gods and emperors had been centuries ago. This led to many abuses, which in their turn provoked the violent reaction of iconoclasm: from A.D. 726 and for over a hundred years, all religious art representing human beings was strictly forbidden. Innumerable works of art, church decorations, illuminated manuscripts, and religious images were ruthlessly destroyed. This is the reason for the gap in our information on Byzantine art prior to the ninth century. It is generally thought that the fanatical image-destroyers were to a large extent influenced by the rigid attitude of Islam, which branded all anthropomorphic representations as idolatry. Orthodoxy was not restored until A.D. 843.

The following three centuries at last saw the true spirit of Byzantium come fully into its own. The relations between religious and imperial art were renewed, and from then on the two developed on strictly parallel lines. A distinctive style of ecclesiastical architecture was evolved, which ultimately became the ideal vehicle for the system of church decoration developed by Byzantine theologians. The ground plan of the new type of church was the Greek cross, i.e., four arms of equal length surmounted at their intersection by a large central dome. The angles between the arms of the cross were filled in with lower vaulted units, thus producing a full square in the ground plan but preserving the cross-shaped space in the superstructure. Three apses were added to the square in the east, and an entrance hall, or narthex, in the west. This type of church remained limited to the East and was rarely taken up in the Latin West, where basilicas were almost always built on the Latin cross plan (i.e., one long arm, nave and aisles, crossed by a shorter arm, the transept).

The most characteristic feature of the Byzantine cross-in-square church is the vaulted superstructure, which can be taken in at a single glance. While the details of the ground plan may vary, the configuration of the vault itself remains invariable; it is the image of the changeless and perpetual celestial world. The cupola itself always dominates the impression, and contains only representations of the holiest persons. Only three subjects were admissable—the Pantocrator (the all-ruler of the Universe), the Ascension, and the descent of the Holy Ghost—though they were hardly ever found side by side in the same building. The conch of the main apse invariably has an icon of the Virgin, either seated or standing; frequently she is attended by angels.

NOTES ON THE ILLUSTRATIONS

108 The drum of the Theotokos church, the smaller of the two churches at the Monastery of Hosios Loukas, *c.* A.D. 1040 (the adjoining katholikon with its mosaics, dedicated to the local saint, is of slightly earlier date, *c.* A.D. 1020). Generally speaking, this church, built on a cross-in-square plan, follows the Constantinopolitan tradition of Middle Byzantine ecclesiastical architecture. But the exuberant ornamental decoration of the exterior is characteristic of Greece. One admires the well-determined proportions of the structure, with its multi-shadow bands of dog-tooth friezes enlivening the surface; the accurate fitting of the masonry; the careful elaboration of detailed ornament. The octagonal drum, an outstandingly beautiful work, is pierced by double windows surmounted by ornamental lion heads and framed by strongly profiled marble slabs with crosses and deeply undercut interlaced ornaments. Colonnettes project at the corners of the drum. At the east end, not visible in this photograph, there is a decoration of cut-brick Kufic letters, a fashion that was particularly popular during the eleventh century. This imitation of Arabic script has its counterpart in the mosaics of the katholikon.

109 Mosaics from the central bay of the narthex of the katholikon of the Monastery of Hosios Loukas. The narthex has its own "heavenly zone" (cf. Daphni); thus the Pantocrator is usually found over the main entrance from the narthex into the church proper.

Christ is represented holding the Gospel Book, which is open, in his left hand, and pointing to it with his right. Saint Peter is depicted on the arch, and, above him in a roundel, Saint Mark. Represented in the vault above Christ, travelling clockwise: first the Virgin Mary, then the Archangel Michael, Saint John Prodromos, and the Archangel Gabriel. Saint Paul may be seen as a counterpart to Saint Peter on the second archway.

This church of Hosios Loukas was consecrated to a local hermit saint, Loukas Stiriotes, who died in A.D. 946 or 949. The church he had erected in A.D. 942 became a holy spot, and pilgrimages were made there to honour the dead saint. This early church was replaced by the present one at the beginning of the eleventh century A.D. The rich decoration of the church consisted of mosaics and a polychrome marble revetment. The church was damaged by an earthquake in A.D. 1659. Some of the mosaics were destroyed and later replaced by frescoes.

Mosaics such as these were formed by placing tiny cubes, or tesserae, in a bed of plaster. They were irregularly set to catch the changing effect of light at different times of the day. In the Middle Byzantine period the background was executed with transparent cubes of glass that enclosed thin sheets of gold, giving the effect of a glittering gold backdrop.

The hieratic style of the Hosios Loukas mosaics reflects the monastic asceticism practised in the seclusion of the mountains near Delphi, and forms an impressive contrast to the aristocratic ease and elegance of the work at Daphni. Though somewhat limited in scope and not of uniformly high standard throughout, this church, which has also preserved most of its marble revetment, can give us an excellent idea of the general effect of a middle Byzantine church completely decorated with mosaics. These mosaics demonstrate the monastic trend in Byzantine art, more straightforward and less sophisticated than

the court art of Daphni. The eleventh century was the great century of monasticism, during which most of the monasteries of Mount Athos were founded or enlarged. The rough, angular, and sometimes downright unlovely figures of Hosios Loukas lack the grace and balance of their counterpart at Daphni, but are a supreme manifestation of the austere monastic spirit of the age.

110 Mosaic depicting the birth of Christ from the Byzantine church at Daphni, on the ancient holy way from Athens to Eleusis.

The church of Daphni was consecrated to the Dormition of the Virgin, one of the twelve great feasts of the Orthodox Church. In the sixth century, a monastery was built on the spot, probably over the ruins of a temple dedicated to Apollo. The present church, a rebuilding of the abandoned monastery, was erected around A.D. 1080 on the Greek cross plan. The interior was decorated with mosaics during the remainder of the eleventh century.

Though of comparatively late date, the mosaics of Daphni are among the purest manifestations of the Hellenistic tradition in Byzantine monumental art and represent a classicistic trend mainly patronized by the emperor and the court in Constantinople—a visual counterpart in Christian garb to the assiduous study of Classical authors and philosophers practised in the schools of the capital.

From the mosaics in the central dome of the church, the beholder's eyes were gradually led towards the decorations of the lower part of the church —the cycle of the twelve great feasts of the Church in the central zone, and the simple figures of saints in the lowest mosaic zone immediately above the marble revetment of the walls (which is no longer preserved at Daphni). Despite the loss of many mosaics and unskillful restoration at the end of the last century, these mosaics still stand out as the finest of their kind preserved in Greece, masterpieces of early Comnenian art.

The scene in this photograph depicting the birth of Christ is perfectly adapted to the curved surface of the niche in which it is contained; unfortunately the left part of the composition is damaged. There is a rugged cave in a pyramid-shaped mountain; in front of the cave, the Child, in swaddling clothes and with a crossed nimbus, lies in a rectangular manger. Behind the manger appear the heads of the ox and ass. The Virgin is shown in a reclining attitude, in front and somewhat to the left of the manger; the upper part of her body is slightly raised, her head almost frontal. Two of the four angels included in the picture bend down to worship Christ; the angel to the left raises his right arm, as if to draw attention to the ray of light that falls upon the Child from Heaven; the one on the extreme right turns to the shepherds to announce to them the birth of the

Saviour. Joseph is seated in the right corner in an attitude of quiet meditation. (These last two figures are not visible in this photograph.) The Mother and Child stand out as the central group, towards which most of the other figures turn or bend; even the shape of the traditional cave and the graceful curves of the mountainous landscape lead the beholder's eyes towards the two protagonists. The figures of the angels with their expressive heads and classical draperies have a peculiar beauty all their own; the draperies fall in long, sweeping curves that echo the rounding and function of the limbs. Some of the folds meet in sharp angles that enliven the surface through the interplay of rhythmical patterns. The colour scheme is rich and brilliant, and at the same time very delicate and refined. As a work of art this mosaic is perhaps somewhat more impersonal than its various counterparts at Hosios Loukas.

111   A view of Mistra during a storm, with the church of Odigitria in the left foreground. The site was first used as a fortress by Guillaume de Ville-hardouin in A.D. 1249; in 1263 he was forced to cede it to the Emperor Michael Palaeologus as ransom for his freedom. The villagers of Lacedemonia (ancient Sparta) came to Mistra and placed themselves under the Emperor's protection; thus the Byzantine city of Mistra had its beginnings. It was the residence of the despot of the Morea (the Peloponnesus), usually a close relative of the reigning emperor. The ruins of the huge palace, which show strong Western influence, are still standing. It became an important cultural center during the fourteenth and fifteenth centuries, a last outpost of dying Hellenism. Its most outstanding resident was the Neoplatonic philosopher Gemistus Pletho. The city lived on under Turkish occupation, but was burned in A.D. 1770 by the Albanians, and from then on abandoned. In recent years the Greek Archeological Service has been restoring it to its ancient glories.

112   Fresco of Saint John baptizing Jesus Christ in the River Jordan from the Church of the Monastery of the Peribleptos (the Protecting Virgin) at Mistra.

This church is decorated with some of the most beautiful frescoes and offers the most complete cycle still preserved at Mistra. The change from mosaic to fresco, almost universal in the Late Byzantine period, was at first due to financial considerations. The system of decoration is still entirely traditional, and repeats the standard arrangement of scenes worked out after the end of iconoclasm to decorate Greek-cross-plan Byzantine churches. The baptism, as one of the twelve great feasts of the Orthodox Church, has one of the places of honour. But the scene is here distinguished by an abundance of narrative detail and picturesque additions: Saint John, standing on the bank of the River Jordan, places his right hand on the head

of Christ. Christ appears to be standing on top of the water, while fish and human beings, perhaps some of his disciples awaiting baptism, swim around him. Saint John's drapery and the body of Christ are seen in terms of calligraphic patterns, while Christ's face is more realistically rendered.   (Middle of the fourteenth century A.D.)

113   A fresco representing the Nativity from the south transept vault of the Church of the Monastery of the Peribleptos at Mistra.

The Virgin is seen in the center of the fresco, in front of the traditional cave, in a wild mountainous landscape. To her left the Christ Child, wrapped in swaddling clothes, lies in his crib, over which appear the heads of the gentle ox and ass. The three Magi approach on horseback from the left, the shepherds to the right. Above, a multitude of angels adore the Child. In scenes of the Nativity in Byzantine art, Saint Joseph is always pictured apart from the Holy Family, since he had not taken part in the divine conception of the Child. Here he sits somewhat disconsolately in the lower right corner.

In frescoes like this, or those of the Divine Liturgy in the apse of the same church, the Byzantine masters approach the expressive power of Giotto himself. These works are the product of great erudition and refinement, permeated by a spirit of true humanism. Their sense of colour is also remarkable. The lyrical tenderness, the fragile grace of these figures make this fresco one of the most beautiful creations of late Byzantine art. (Middle of the fourteenth century A.D.)

114   The Chapel of the Trinity in the Monastery of the Great Lavra on Mount Athos.

The layout of Middle Byzantine monasteries reflects a tradition that probably goes back to the Early Byzantine period. A fortified wall encloses a wide courtyard in the center of which stands the monastery church. The cells of the monks, aligned in long rows against the enclosing walls, face the courtyard. The refectory (the *trapeza*) occupies one side of the courtyard; it is a long hall, aisleless and terminated by an apse. There is either one long table with benches running along the central axis, or a number of semicircular tables (*sigmata*) standing along the walls of the refectory (see plate 116).

The Chapel of the Trinity in this monastery is a good example of the overornateness of Greek ecclesiastical interiors. The door of the iconostasis was made during the fifteenth and sixteenth centuries. The reliquaries and icons date from various periods, many going back to the eleventh and twelfth centuries. One wonders whether the interiors of ancient Greek temples were as cluttered with votive gifts as many of their Byzantine descendants are.

The library of this monastery contains five thousand volumes and more than two thousand manu-

scripts, some evangelistaries dating from the eleventh and twelfth centuries.

115 The Monastery of Dochyriu founded in A.D. 1034 by Euthymius. This idiorrhythmic monastery on Mount Athos, with its fortresslike tower rising from a clustered group of houses, could well form a tiny Italian hill town. The solemn cypress trees form a beautiful and dignified background. It is one of the most picturesque monasteries on the Holy Mountain.

Through the centuries, the monasteries were endowed by emperors and others, and received precious gifts, often outstanding and unique works of art, icons, or illuminated manuscripts, or great stretches of valuable land. Many manuscripts, jewelled bookcovers, etc., can still be identified as donations given by individual emperors. Only members of the male sex are permitted within the holy area; hens, cows, and women are prohibited.

116 The refectory, or dining room, of the Monastery of the Great Lavra, the earliest of all the twenty monastic foundations on the Holy Mountain.

Next to the katholikon (community church), the refectory (the trapeza) is the most important liturgical center of the Athos monasteries. Dining in the refectory is not thought of as an interruption of the service: the monks enter it while singing psalms, and eat in silence while they listen to stories of saints' lives read aloud to them. Frescoes of religious subjects on the walls evoke an atmosphere similar to that of the church itself. Thus, the katholikon and the trapeza are the two liturgical centers of the monasteries, complementing each other. Frequently this is even expressed in the ground plan, in that they face each other symmetrically across the courtyard.

Founded in A.D. 963 by Saint Athanasius (his true name was Abramos of Trebizond) this monastery resembled a fortified village. The lovely frescoes in the chapel of St. Nicholas are signed by "the hand of the most worthless Frangos Castellanos of Thebes in Boeotia," and dated A.D. 1560.

The convents were divided into two classes. The cenobitic order was first established in Egypt, and then taken up by St. Basil the Great. It followed the usual type of orthodox monastic life, a strict rule imposing certain restraints, especially of fasting. The second order, the idiorrhythmic, was less strict. The monks could acquire property and live on their personal resources which they could, in turn, bequeath to other monks. The idiorrhythmic monks first established themselves on Athos in the late fourteenth century. In sharp contrast to the cenobitic, their cells were often lavishly decorated with furniture, rugs, and works of art, and they often employed servants to care for their earthly needs. The Great Lavra belonged to the idiorrhythmic order, hence the beautifully decorated refectory.

117 The white church of Paraportiani, one of the more than three hundred and sixty churches and chapels on the Island of Mykonos. These were constructed in comparatively recent times by sailors grateful for their prosperity and hopeful that the Lord and the Virgin Mary would continue their benefices and protect them from the perils of the sea. In antiquity, these sailors would certainly have been initiated into the Samothracian mysteries.

118 The Monastery of Chrysopighi on the island of Siphnos. Built in recent times on a promontory, this monastery gives the impression of being on an island of its own. The Greek genius for selecting dramatically beautiful sites on which to erect temples and churches still survives. Although the majority of Greek churches were constructed on the central plan, there is great variety in exterior appearance.

119 View of the city of Phira at sunset on the Cycladic island of Santorini (Thera). The domes of its beautiful churches glow in the light reflected in the crater bay, in the center of which can be seen the ominous black volcanic island of Nea Kaimeni, still active.

Santorini has been inhabited since some two thousand years before Christ. She was colonized by the Phoenicians and then by the Dorians, and was an important naval base throughout antiquity.

The two houses illuminated to the left of the lower church resemble the Minoan faïence votive plaques of houses, thus perpetuating a thirty-six-hundred-year-old tradition. The ancient, traditional rectangular house architecture of the Cycladic islands contrasts with the comparatively new round forms of Cycladic church architecture.

120 The village Chora on the Cycladic island of Seriphos, illumined in the bluish-silver light of the moon. Such a village, clinging to the side of a mountain, with flat-topped roofs, small windows, and stuccoed, whitewashed walls, could be the model of an ancient town. Only the church on the slope of the hill places it in Christian times.

121 The back of a caryatid on the porch of the maidens, the Erechtheion:

O Attic shape! Fair attitude! with brede
Of marble men and maidens overwrought, . . .
Thou, silent form! dost tease us out of thought
As doth eternity. . . .
  When old age shall this generation waste,
    Thou shalt remain, in midst of other woe
  Than ours, a friend to man, to whom thou say'st,
"Beauty is truth, truth beauty,—that is all
    Ye know on earth, and all ye need to know."
      —John Keats, "Ode on a Grecian Urn"

INDEX

(Plate numbers are in bold-face type.)